STANDING ALONE

16 Stand Alone Dramatic Monologues
8 monologues for women
8 monologues for men

Melville Lovatt

Running time for each monologue
7 - 10 minutes

TSL Drama

Published in Great Britain in 2016
By TSL (Drama) Publications, Rickmansworth

Copyright © 2016 Melville Lovatt

Images courtesy of sattva at FreeDigitalPhotos.net

ISBN / 978-1-911070-33-7

Rights of performance

DEDICATION

To my wife Lynda, daughter Anna and son Simon

Melville Lovatt

Melville Lovatt is an award winning playwright and monologue writer. His work has been widely performed in smaller theatres throughout London. A number of his plays have won awards:

The Powers That Be won The Sussex Playwrights Club 1st Prize for best full length play.

Small Mercies, a full length play, won The Jack Langford Memorial Award and The Derek Lomas Memorial Award.

Two one act plays, *The Grave* and *The Kiss*, were short-listed for The Diane Raffle Award.

Melville Lovatt is a member of The Pinner Writers Group and is currently President of Harrow Writers Circle. He lives in Hatch End, Northwest London.

Full Length Plays

Small Mercies	Comedy-Drama	4M	2F
The Powers That Be	Thriller	3M	3F + 1 boy
Visiting Time	Family Drama	3M	2F
Desperate Measures	Dark Comedy	3M	1F

One Act Plays

Accommodation	Tragicomedy	4M	1F
The Lamp	Comedy-Drama	1M	1F
The Distressed Table	Comedy-Drama	1M	1F + Voiceover (F)
The Boomerang	Comedy-Drama	3M	1Boy + Voiceover (F)
The Kiss	Thriller	2M	1F
The Weekend	Drama	2M	1F
The Grave	Drama	2M	

Duologue

Bedtime Story	Drama	1M	1F

Monologue Collections

Standing Alone	Comedy-Drama	8M	8F

All enquiries to TSL Publications: www.tslbooks.uk

Author's Note

The monologues in this collection are independent of each other and can be performed individually or collectively.

STANDING ALONE

Anita is dreading husband Ron's retirement.

Making Adjustments

Making Adjustments was first presented at
East Lane Theatre, Wembley, London

on 23 August 2015
with the following cast:

Anita ... **Linda Hampson**

Winner of The National Operatic & Dramatic
Association London Region Performance Showcase
Festival Award
NODA 23rd June 2018

with the following cast:

Anita ... **Linda Hampson**
Directed by Melville Lovatt

Author's production note

Where indicated, the lights should quickly fade and snap back on to denote a brief passing of time.

Anita – *A still attractive woman in her early sixties. (Lights up. Anita stands, addresses audience.)*

ANITA: To tell you the truth, I've been dreading this time.

Ron's retirement, that is, for quite a while, now.

Oh, I know it's selfish to feel like this. But that's how I *do* feel.

What can I say? The thing is, I've got used to having my own space.

But Ron seems intent on *invading* my space. He has so many plans to keep us both *active,* I'm not sure I'll have any space left.

(Pause.)

My friend, Doris, says it's all about making adjustments.

It's alright for *her.* For her to say that.

She never really had to make adjustments at all.

Before *he* could retire, her husband dropped dead.

(Pause.)

Oh, what am I saying? Poor, poor woman.

It's got to be harder adjusting to *that.*

In her husband's case, though, it *was* to be expected.

(Softer, confidential.) What I mean is, he drank whisky out of his ears.

(Pause.)

I've been retired for two years, now. I don't miss working in retail one bit.

Right now, I like my life just as it is. Some people may say it's a bit dull.

So what? I've spent my entire life pleasing other people.

Now I feel it's time to just please myself. Oh, I know this may seem uninspiring to some, but I tend to like *quiet* things. Bird watching.

Reading. Reading romantic novels and poems.

When I've done all my chores, there's nothing I like better than to put my feet up with a good book, a nice cup of coffee and a bar of chocolate. A Turkish Delight or a Walnut Whip.

(Pause.)

They're having Ron's retirement party tonight at a posh restaurant in the centre of town. The Prison Service are paying for it all.

I'm led to believe there'll be no expense spared.

Yes, the Prison Governor and his wife will be there.

She looks down on everyone from a great height.

One or two more bigwigs might be there as well.

(Looks at watch.) The table's been booked for seven.

(Quick fade.

Lights up.)

All in all, I suppose it was going *well.*

Everyone agreed the food was tip-top.

The Governor made a very nice speech thanking Ron for his service as a Prison Officer. For all the good work he's done through the years.

Then Ron got to his feet and made a speech, too, thanking the Governor for all *his* support.

'I've enjoyed The Prison Service,' Ron said.

'There's been ups and downs but, by and large, I've been happy. Fulfilled. I feel I've made a contribution.

Feel I've played my part in keeping things ... s*afe.*

If I had my time over, I'd do it all again.'

When he said this, I *knew* he'd had too much to drink.

The point is, Ron always *hated* his job.

He never stopped moaning from morning 'til night.

'The thing is,' he always said, *(Imitates Ron's voice.)* 'There's no escaping the fact, *a Prison Officer is in prison, too.*

He's a prisoner, himself. He's banged up, himself.

At the end of the day, there's no changing that.'

(Pause.)

I told him a million times to change jobs.

'If you're *so* fed up, just do something else.'

But he didn't. He did nothing. *(Imitates Ron's voice.)* 'There's my pension to think of. My pension to think of. What about that?'

That's all he could think of. His pension at the end.

(Imitates Ron's voice.) 'Without the pension, what

will we do?'

(Pause.)

Well, Ron finished his speech and then he sat down.

As I said, I knew there was something very wrong.

Him waxing so lyrical over the job ...

The next thing was, he'd gone white as a sheet.

Well, it has to be said, Ron's just not used to drinking.

Before the meal, people kept buying him drinks and the waiters were pouring wine right through the meal.

All the time, the Governor's wife kept prattling on ...

She's one of those women who, once she starts talking, she can't seem to stop herself. Know what I mean?

She just went on and on. *(Imitates Governor's wife's affected voice.)* 'How important it is in retirement to have a range of interests to pursue.'

Ron was turning green, now. I could see what was coming but it happened so quickly. There was nothing I could do.

(Small ironic chuckle.) When it happened, she stopped talking.

Started yelling instead. There was pandemonium.

God, what a mess! Her dress was a write-off.

Such a lovely dress, too.

(Pause.)

She's sending Ron the bill.

(Quick fade.

Lights up.)

So today's the second day of Ron's retirement.

He spent the first day recovering in bed from the farewell party.

What can you say? *(Shrugs.)* Best forgotten, I suppose.

Just one of those things.

(Pause.)

Well, today we're both going out to play golf.

We've never played golf before in our lives.

But Ron's booked us lessons. Driving Range Lessons.

He thinks Ten Pin Bowling is a good idea, too.

He's a whole range of *do-able* activities lined up.

Yes, high on his list is *The Busy Bees.*

That's a Rambling Club. Ron say's we've got to keep fit.

He's also enrolled us both down at the gym.

(Quick fade.

Lights up.)

The golf lessons went well. I quite enjoyed it.

The instructor was a dishy young man called Klaus.

He was Austrian or German. About half my age.

Oh, I *am* awful, aren't I? I told myself off.

'*Concentrate on the golf,*' I said. I *did* try my best.

But I found I became captivated by his swing.

(Dreamily.) Whenever he demonstrated how it should be done, I found myself thinking ...

(Suddenly stops herself, slaps wrist once, hard.)

Stop it! Enough!

(Pause.)

Meanwhile, things weren't going too well for Ron.

He couldn't seem to get the hang of it at all.

In the end, Klaus told him to watch *my* technique.

'Watch your wife,' he said. 'She's getting it right.'

It wasn't very tactful for Klaus to say that.

From this point on, I could see Ron was narked.

Klaus left us for a while to practice our swings.

Try as he may, Ron couldn't get it right.

He's too perfectionist. That's always been his trouble.

We were only supposed to hit fifty balls *max,* but Ron, in his frustration, hit a hundred.

Now he seems to have damaged his shoulder ...

(Quick fade.

Lights up.)

Today we went to play Ten Pin Bowling.

Ron insisted he was okay to do this.

He's arranged physiotherapy for his left shoulder.

(Imitates Ron's voice.) 'My right shoulder's unaffected,' he said. 'And, as I'm right handed, there's nothing to stop me making a record number of strikes.'

I didn't know what this meant. Turned out a strike

is when you knock the skittles down all in one go.

So off we toddled to the bowling alley.

The last thing in the world I wanted to do.

But anything for a quiet life, eh?

He kept on and on, and so I gave it a go.

(Pause.)

As it happened, I turned out to be quite good at it.

I found I quickly got the hang of it. Right?

It just seemed, to me, like a very simple game.

In our second game, I got three strikes in a row.

Well, Ron couldn't understand it. 'Beginners luck,' he said. 'Beginners luck, Anita. That's all it is.'

At first, he was pleased, but when I kept winning, he seemed to go into a bit of a sulk.

And then who should appear in the next lane, but Doris? New boyfriend, as well.

Much younger than her.

She saw me first and shouted across.

I'd just picked a bowl up when she yelled out.

As I turned around, surprised, the bowl slipped from my hand and ... oh well, the least said, the better.

(Quick Fade.

Lights Up.)

In my humble opinion, the best inventions are always very simple in material and design.

Take the Zimmer Frame, for instance.

What is it after all? Just an aluminium walking

frame. Right? But just *think* of its benefits to millions of people. Without the Zimmer Frame, where would they be?

When I watch Ron, I marvel. His foot's getting better.

At the moment, he's wearing a large plaster shoe.

But the Zimmer Frame means he can move around the house. It's a blessing, he's not just stuck in his chair.

(Pause.)

Even so, he was getting bored and ratty.

(Imitates Ron's voice.) 'It's worse than being in prison, this is.'

Doris said, 'The best thing is to keep him busy.'

So I've got him doing some light housework, now.

Got him doing some dusting. And I've shown him how to cook. Today I've got him making Toad In The Hole.

Who knows? Perhaps cooking may prove his *real* forte?

He's shown an aptitude for it straightaway.

I can't keep him out of the kitchen at all.

He's insisting on cooking the Sunday roast.

(Pause.)

I personally never liked cooking, much.

I can take it or leave it, if you know what I mean?

So it suits me fine if Ron wants to take over.

If he fancies himself as a master chef, ... *great!*

(Pause.)

Last Tuesday, I must say he took me by surprise.

I'd been out visiting my sister in Leeds.

I came home to a candlelit dinner with wine and Lasagne, followed by Italian ice cream.

(Pause.)

Who knows where these romantic dinners will lead?

He seems to be getting quite amorous again.

There's been nothing for ages but Doris told me last week there's a new pill on the market which helps men to *perform.*

(Pause.)

I suppose you could say things are *perking up.*

But I have trouble feeling amorous, myself.

Let's face it, how many women are turned on by a man with a Zimmer and a large plaster shoe?

(Pause.)

Still, with Ron in the kitchen, I'm playing more golf.

I've got into it. I'm playing for the Ladies Team, now.

Klaus tells me it's time we had a *proper* game, together.

That it's time I ... took him on.

(Fade.)

'That's what it was. A newspaper wall.'

The Wall

The Wall was first presented by
Tin Shed Theatre Company at
The Davenham Players Theatre,
Davenham, Northwich

on 28 April 2011
with the following cast:

Vera ... **Denise Barry**

Vera – *A still attractive woman in her early sixties.*

(Lights up. VERA sits at a garden patio table. She sips orange juice, staring at the sky. She puts down the glass, stares ahead.)

VERA: No use moping is it? What can you do? No choice. You've just got to get on with it? Right? No alternative is there? No. None at all.

(Pause.)

Well, that's not strictly true …

(Pause.)

The alternative is to *not* get on with it.

Just pack it in. Just call it a day.

Drown yourself. Shoot yourself. Jump off Beachy Head.

(Pause.)

Not my style at all.

(Pause.)

(She sips orange juice, puts down glass.

She stares straight ahead.)

(Pause.)

Besides, if I did that, *(Points out front.)* how would they cope?

Who would look after Bobo and Squeak?

(Stands, shouts.) Bobo! Leave Squeak alone! You naughty pussy!

Leave her alone! Do you hear me?! Shoo!

18

(Sits again.) There's Robert as well ... such a silly rabbit.

Who would look after Robert if I wasn't here?

No, it's out of the question. Complete non starter.

No, ... not my style at all.

(Pause.)

Of course, Jeff never liked Bobo and Squeak.

He wasn't a lover of animals. No.

He was quite fond of Robert, I think. Oh yes.

(Small chuckle.) But he hated cats. Didn't like them at all.

(Pause.)

It's been two years now since Jeff passed away.

Time's flown by, really. Well, in some ways it has but in other ways ... well ... the evenings go slow ... it's the evenings, mostly.

Just seem ... so quiet.

(Pause.)

Bear in mind, though, it was quiet with Jeff.

It's no quieter, really, than when he was here.

He was not one for talking, to put it mildly.

He couldn't bear anyone rabbiting on.

I mean, don't get me wrong. We did used to talk.

About once a month, we talked ... quite a bit.

It was just ... most evenings ... most evenings, he ... well ...

(Pause.)

He just liked to read.

(Pause.)

Liked to read his paper. His Sunday paper.

He'd buy it on Sunday to read through the week.

Each night he'd sit reading a different section.

The main news first, and then the review, then the sport, then the business supplement. Yes. He'd be hidden behind it.

Night after night. And sometimes it felt like a wall between us.

That's what it was. A newspaper wall.

And although it was paper, it didn't seem like paper.

It didn't ... didn't seem like paper at all.

The wall went up at seven and just ... stayed up.

(Pause.)

Night after night.

(Pause.)

But I wouldn't want you thinking it was always like that.

It was very different in our younger days. Yes.

Well, when all's said and done, I *was* a top model.

And not just in London. In Paris and Rome.

All the top designers ... I've modelled for them all.

Versace. Chanel. Yves Saint Laurent.

That's how I met Jeff. He was in the same business.

A fashion photographer, just starting out.

His photographs of me helped launch his career.

(Emphatically.) His photographs of *me* helped make

his name.

Oh, in those days, I had his undivided attention.

He couldn't photograph me often enough.

His favourite model. He told me I was.

His own little Princess. His Belle of the ball.

Yes, in those days, I was always very much centre stage.

It was very different, then.

(Pause.)

It's true we were never very *active.*

Not *over active,* if you know what I mean?

Truth be told, I preferred a nice bar of chocolate.

A Walnut Whip or a Cadbury's Whole nut.

But, yes, ... we did used to ... two nights a week.

(Pause.)

Sometimes three.

(Pause.)

And then ... that stopped. Don't remember when.

Jeff just said, 'I think we'll give it a rest.'

The thing is, though, I didn't really want it to stop.

Not stop completely. Like it did.

I mean to say, a bar of chocolate's all very nice, but everyone needs ... a bit of a change. A bit of ... affection.

That's all I was after.

(Pause.)

Once in a while?

(Pause.)

Oh, I did my best to *rekindle* his interest.

Oh yes, I *did* try, but he'd made up his mind.

He'd had enough of this *horizontal dancing.*

That's what he called it. *(Ponders briefly.)* I hadn't thought of it like that. A *funny* term, really, when you come to think of it. Well, from then on ... the newspaper wall.

Until one day he said, 'The oak trees needed pruning.'

Looking back, I thought it was odd at the time.

The thing was, he always hated gardening.

It was all he could do to just mow the lawn.

Then, out of the blue, he starts pruning the trees.

Yes, looking back, I thought it was odd.

God knows though, the trees really did need pruning.

The lower branches, mainly, were out of control.

They were overlapping our back neighbour's wall.

They needed a tree surgeon, really, still ...

Jeff said he could do it. Got a book from the library.

I've got to admit I was quite impressed with the way he tackled it, day after day. He just seemed to take on a new lease of life.

And, yes, I was pleased. I always liked gardening and now Jeff was taking an interest as well. Even doing some weeding and planting flowers for me. At last a shared interest!

Yes, something ... shared.

(Pause.)

The day that it happened, he'd been out on the ladder, pruning the last tree by the back wall.

I called out, 'Dinner's ready!' A Sunday, it was.

I'd made a nice roast beef and Yorkshire pud.

No response. So I shouted. Called out again.

Still no response. He was high up the tree. He was up in the tree.

That's why he couldn't hear me.

(Pause.)

Well, that's what I thought.

(Pause.)

'Must have lost his footing.' That's what they said.

'Fell twenty feet, smashed his head on a rock.'

They thought he'd have died more or less straight away.

(Pause.)

They seemed certain of that.

(Pause.)

Of course, they didn't see the camera. I made sure they didn't.

It wasn't their business, anyway, right?

It was none of their business. There was no need.

No need to let them see it at all.

(Pause.)

I know one or two people found it strange I should scatter Jeff's ashes there by the back wall. But I thought it was fitting.

It was Jeff's favourite place. It seemed to me he was happiest there.

There were so many photographs. Twenty at least of her in her bikini and some of her nude. Of course, she had no idea he was taking them. No. Sunbathing, that's all. She had no idea ...

(Suddenly stands.) Now Bobo! I've told you! Leave Jeff alone!

You wouldn't like it if someone piddled on you!

Anyone would think I encouraged you to do it.

Squeak! Come away, now! Shoo!

(Fade)

May recalls an egg and spoon race and its unexpected consequences.

Egg And Spoon

Egg & Spoon was first presented as part of
the Harrow Drama Festival
by Belmont Theatre Company at
The Travellers Theatre, Harrow,

on 8 July 2003
with the following cast:

May … **Anita Stevens**

Winner of The National Operatic & Dramatic
Association London Region Performance Showcase
Festival Award
NODA 23rd June 2018

with the following cast:

May … **Kim Wedler**
Directed by Melville Lovatt

May – *A woman of sixty.*

(Lights up. MAY sits in a fireside chair. She sips tea, refers to audience.)

MAY: Believe it or not, I remember a time when my mum was affectionate towards me. Yes. Yes, she used to read to me. Read me stories.

She would sometimes let me sit on her knee, and she'd cuddle me.

Kiss me. Sometimes sing me a song.

(Pause.)

But all this was when I was *very* little. Long before the egg and spoon.

(Long pause.)

I remember it being a glorious day. A perfect day. Not a cloud in the sky.

The first sports day we'd had when the weather was good.

Every year before that, it was windy. Or rained.

Yes, a Wednesday it was. I remember that because my dad had half a day off.

Wednesday afternoon. Yes. The shops used to close then.

(Smiles.) I can see him now. *(Small chuckle.)* He wore his best suit.

Mum wore her best coat. Matching hat and scarf.

In those days, you see, people used to dress up.

People used to dress up a lot more than now.

(Offers plate of biscuits.) Are you *sure* you won't have a biscuit?

(Pause.)

I was ten years old. All the parents were there in their best bib and tuckers, as dad used to say. All the teachers ... the headmaster ... what was his name?

Mr Bil ... *Mr Bilby.* Bilby. That's right. He was there, in his gown.

His cap and gown. Cap and gown on sports day? Real show-off, he was.

And his wife was there too. She was one of those women ... always seemed like she had a bad smell up her nose. And bossy? You bet!

A bossier person you'd never meet. Oh yes, she wore the pants.

Mr Bilby was a bully but she bullied *him.* It was so funny watching her order him around. Another thing was, she made all the announcements on the loudspeaker. Such a lah-de-dah voice!

All us girls used to giggle as she's bark it all out.

(Imitates voice.) 'Would Michael Johnston of class 3B pull up his socks and straighten his tie?! Would Annabel Quince put her school blazer on and adjust her blouse this minute?!'

(Small chuckle.) Well, anyway, I was in just one race. The egg and spoon.

That was all I could get. I wasn't fast enough for the hundred yards or the marathon. They said my legs were too short.

So that was my race. Just the egg and spoon. No importance attached to it, really. At all. 'A nothing race with nobodies in it.'

That's what I heard Bilby say to his wife.

Your team only got one point, if you won it.

All the other races, you got at least three.

Well, the race was to take place at three o'clock but when the time came, they couldn't find the spoons. They had plenty of eggs but they'd lost all the spoons! They'd gone missing. Gone walkies out of the tent.

I remember thinking they *were* nice spoons. Quite elaborate.

Far too elaborate for ... well, an egg and spoon race.

Anyway, well, an announcement was made by Mrs Bilby.

(Imitates voice.) 'The egg and spoon will now be the final race.

I'm sure it will prove a fun end to the day.'

Yes, that's what she said. *A fun end to the day.*

Then she sent me to the village to buy some more spoons.

When I got back, most of the races had been run.

There were only two left. Just the marathon and mine.

Everybody was excited. So excited. We'd never beaten Mr Keane's class before and here we were now with the points all level if we won the marathon. And win it, we did!

Well, the crowd went wild. Mum went *very* wild.

I remember she threw her hat high in the air.

Stupid thing to do, really. It landed in the mud.

A write-off. She never wore it again ...

Well, the next thing I knew, it was starter's orders.

The nothing race wasn't *the nothing race,* now.

The nothing race was the most important race.

The race which decided which class won the day.

Starter's orders. 'On your marks! Get set! Go!'

I couldn't have got off to a much better start.

I was way out in front right from the word go.

All the other girls just kept on dropping their eggs but mine stayed on and I ran and I ran and the crowd were cheering and roaring away. 'Come on 3B! Come on 3B!'

I was winning but they were catching me up.

I could sense they were close. They were closing the gap but my egg stayed on and theirs fell off again and not far away I could see the tape. Yes! Yes, the finishing tape!

They were closing again but I ran and I ran my heart pounding like mad. 'Come on 3B! Come on 3B! Hold on! Hold on!'

They were closing the gap but the tape was there!

The tape was there! And before I knew it, I'd won! I'd won!

And they patted me, kissed me, shook me by the hand and hoisted me up and paraded me around and I saw my mum and dad all smiles, just beaming and waving, so happy and proud.

And I was so happy. Happier, then, in those few minutes, than I've ever been since. Those few minutes were magic.

Just being the hero. The winning hero for once in my life ...

(Evenly.) Sometimes I can blot out all that happened next.

(Pause.)

Sometimes I can't.

(Pause.)

It started with a whistle. A long, piercing whistle.

We couldn't see who was blowing it at first, then the sound got nearer and we saw Mr Keane storming towards us.

He was just like a mad bull.

He stopped blowing the whistle and pointed to me.

I was still being held aloft in the air.

Then he held up a spoon with an egg glued on it.

'Perhaps your hero can explain this to me!

Perhaps she can tell us *why* she felt she had to *cheat* to win the race!'

Everybody went quiet. They lowered me to the ground.

I stared at the spoon with the egg glued on and I couldn't ... couldn't speak. The words wouldn't come out.

'Admit it! You cheated! Admit it! Come on!'

And the next thing I knew, there was Bilby and his wife.

They were trying their best to calm Mr Keane down but he wouldn't calm down and he started shouting.

'I can't stand cheating! This girl is a cheat!'

And I saw my mum at the front of the crowd, upset now.

She was starting to cry.

'This girl is a cheat! This girl is a cheat!'

Those words have followed me down through the years.

Then my dad stepped forward. It was just like when Henry Cooper knocked down Cassius Clay.

Mr Keane went down like a sack of potatoes.

I'll never forget the look in his eyes.

There was blood ... blood everywhere. Blood from his nose.

Then the police came. Took dad away.

(Pause.)

Mr Keane didn't press charges, to give him his due.

He could have had dad charged with assault but he didn't press charges. Didn't have him charged.

(Pause.)

We were grateful for that.

(Pause.)

It wasn't the sports day. That wasn't the reason.

It's true dad died two days after that, but he had a condition.

A heart condition.

(Pause.)

A defective valve.

(Pause.)

Mum never said so, in so many words, but I know what she thought. I know she blamed me.

But she had no right to blame me at all.

(Pause.)

No right at all.

(Pause.)

It wasn't the sports day killed my dad.

But mum convinced herself that it was.

(Emphatic.) The point was, dad was living on borrowed time.

(Through brief sobbing.) It wasn't the sports day. It wasn't ... my fault.

(Quickly composed again.) I didn't ... didn't cheat.

Didn't knowingly cheat.

The spoon was handed me with the egg on and the next thing I knew it was starter's orders.

STARTER'S VOICE: *(Over loudspeaker.)* On your marks! Get set! Go!

(Crowd heard, distantly, cheering the race as the lights slowly fade.)

Suggested Sound Effect

Starter's voice and crowd cheering with slight echo, suggesting distant past.

Author's Note

In the event of sound effects not being used, MAY to also read Starter's Voice dialogue.

STANDING ALONE

Christine pays three visits to her husband Vincent's grave.

Three Visits To Vincent

Author's Production Note

Where indicated, the lights should quickly fade and snap back on to denote a brief passing of time.

Christine – *A woman in her early fifties.*

(Lights Up. A Cemetery. CHRISTINE stands by a grave.
Pause.
She addresses the grave.)

CHRISTINE: I had *another* dream last night.

Dreamt about a giraffe. I wasn't on safari or anything. No.

The giraffe had escaped. Escaped from a zoo.

(Pause.)

From London zoo.

(Pause.)

That was my guess anyway. That's where I was.

In London, alone on a double-decker bus.

The bus was stuck in traffic. The giraffe just *appeared,* pressed its face to the window, waiting to be fed.

So I opened the window and started to feed him.

I'd just done my shopping, so I fed him some crisps.

Salt and vinegar first, then cheese and onion.

He seemed to like the cheese and onion best.

He wolfed down three bags in no time at all.

But then he became very desperate for a drink.

His long tongue hanging out was a dry as a bone.

And his eyes were so sorrowful. So ... so sad.

(Pause.)

There were lots of people on the pavement, watching.

They all started shouting, 'Give him a drink!'
'I have no water with me!' I shouted back.

But they wouldn't believe me. They turned very aggressive.

'We know you've got water! Give him a drink!

You miserable cow! Go on, give him a drink!'

Well, what could I do? I *had* to do something.

I had to give him *something* to drink.

So I rummaged in my bag, found a tube of ...
well, ... when all's said and done, it *is* water-based ... so I gave his two squirts.

Two squirts, that's all. Two squirts of ... *(softer)* K Y Jelly.

(Pause.)

At first he seemed to really enjoy it.

I saw a big smile break out on his face.

The crowd roared approval. Started to applaud.

Thank God, I was thinking. I've done something *right*.

(Pause.)

The mistake I made was giving him more.

Not a lot. I just gave him two more squirts.

Four squirts was too much. If I'd just stopped at two ...

From then on, things took a turn for the worst.

(Pause.)

There was really no warning. No warning at all.

One minute the giraffe was as right as rain and the next he just turned as white as a sheet. I could see there was something ... something not right.

(Pause.)

He was sick ... quite a lot. Then he sort of ... well ... he seemed like he was drunk ... staggered off towards Hyde Park.

One man began shouting. Going berserk.

'Whose gonna pay me to have my suit cleaned ?!

Whose gonna pay to have this bloody suit cleaned?!'

Then a woman started crying.

'That's my best dress ruined!

I'll never be able to wear it again!'

They all started to point at me. 'She's to blame!

It was all her fault! We'll make *her* pay!'

And the next thing was, they were climbing the stairs of the bus. They were coming to get me!

(Pause.)

That's when I woke up. Woke up in a sweat.

I think I screamed out. Yes, I'm sure ... I *did*.

For a moment, ... split second ... I thought you were there. Just *there*. In our bed. Lying next to me.

(Pause.)

If you *had* been there, you'd have found a connection.

You'd have found some comforting explanation for the dream. Said something like, 'Ah! It was last night's TV!

You were watching David Attenborough before you came to bed!' I can see you now, pointing ... pointing to the telly. Then you'd say, 'There's a lesson to be learned from all this. And the lesson's staring us both in the face.'

'What lesson?' I'd ask.

You would pause, then you'd say, 'Never feed a giraffe K Y Jelly.'

(Pause.)

The strange thing was, you were a hopeless listener.

You never listened to anything I said.

Except when I was telling you about my dreams.

Then you really *did* listen. Listened like a child.

Like a child being told a story.

Yes ... you told me once, you felt closest to me, then.

(Pause.)

I loved *you* most, then.

(Pause.)

Since you passed away ... (*Stops, considers.) Passed away.*

A nice phrase, isn't it? *Passed away.*

Much nicer than saying *he's died, popped his clogs,*

or *Vincent has left the building.* Come on!

If you'd only left the building, I'd have found you outside by the back door, having a smoke.

(Pause.)

Tracey keeps saying, 'It's time you moved on.'

But what does that mean exactly? *Move on?*

What it means to her is meeting lots of men.

She keeps saying, 'Why don't you try internet dating?

Or if you don't fancy that, why not just get a dog?

You'll meet lots of men, just walking their dogs.'

She was man mad even when her husband was alive ...

But you wouldn't mind, would you?

If I met someone else?

(Pause.)

You *wouldn't* mind? Would you?

(Quick Fade.

Lights Up. As before. Three weeks later.)

Tracey's son gave me a dog, last Thursday.

A little Jack Russell. I named him Rex.

Quite a cute little dog, just ten inches tall.

Trouble is, he's fearless. Absolutely fearless.

He thinks nothing of taking on much bigger dogs.

Like, we'd only been out for a walk five minutes when we saw a man walking a large Alsatian.

They were walking straight towards us.

As they drew closer, I noticed the man was about my age. He was quite … dare I say it?

Quite … quite dishy, with a lovely head of silver grey hair and an unlined face with no bags at all.

Must have had a facelift. Still, so what?

(Pause.)

As it happened, this meeting was a *very* mixed blessing.

I never want to see *this* man again.

His Alsatian barked once. Just a short sharp bark.

Then Rex jumped at him, spoiling for a fight. The man yelled out, 'For God's sake, what's wrong with your dog?! Madam, can't you keep your dog under control?!'

Incredibly pompous, calling me madam.

I went right off him, there and then.

I pointed out to him *his* dog had barked first.

'That was just an Alsatian's friendly greeting,' he said.

An Alsatian's friendly greeting? You could have fooled me! There was no denying, though, Rex was the aggressor. In the end, we managed to separate the dogs.

Not before the man had shouted, 'You should have him put down!' By the time I got home, I was *really* stressed out. Then I looked in the mirror and heard my dad's voice. I haven't heard my dad's voice for ten years, since he died. 'Have you noticed,' he was saying, 'After a while, people with dogs start to look like them'? Well … I gave this some thought and it *did* seem to me that the people I'd seen out walking their dogs ...

Well, anyway, I decided dogs just weren't for *me*. Yesterday, Tracey's son took Rex back.

(Quick Fade.

Lights Up. As before. Three Weeks Later.)

It's been five years *today*. Do you realise that?

Exactly five years today.

(Pause.)

Do you realise that? No, of course you don't.

How could you? You're bloody well dead.

(Pause.)

I haven't been with anyone else in that time.

I've become completely celibate. *(Small chuckle.)* Yes.

So celibate, I've almost forgotten what it's like.

I'm lonely. Bored. Bored out of my mind.

It's not the same, doing the walks that we did.

It's not the same, going for walks on my own.

There's days when I don't see anyone at all.

Days when I don't see a soul.

(Pause.)

(Suddenly emphatic ,quite angry.) I refuse to feel guilty.

It wasn't my fault. I refuse to accept the blame, do you hear? Okay, so I *was* a bit materialistic.

No more than the *average* woman. *Come on.*

All those dreams of flash cars and villas abroad I

used to tell you about ... that's all they *were*. *Dreams.*

They weren't ... weren't *me*. They weren't *really me*.

You must have realised that?

(Pause.)

It was *your* decision to do what you did.

If I'd known, I'd have stopped you. I had no idea ...

There was no ... no sign of ... you gave me no clue ...

(Pause.)

I refuse to feel *guilt*.

(Pause.)

You didn't have to do it. You stupid sod.

(Pause.)

You didn't *have* to do *that*.

(Pause.)

I mean, what was the sentence?

Three years at the most?

With remission for good behaviour, just two.

Two years would have flown by in no time at all.

Everything passes. *Everything.*

You ... you weren't the first bank manager with fingers in the till. You weren't the first and you won't be the last. We could have gone away, when you came out.

Could have gone away somewhere, where nobody knew.

(Emphatic.) We could have started ... started again!

(Angry, begins to sob.) We could have made a new start!

(She sobs.

The sobbing stops.

She quickly wipes her eyes.

Pause.)

(Quietly.) I've got to go, now.

They'll be closing the gates.

I'll come again towards the end of the month.

I expect I'll have had a few more crazy dreams.

I'll tell you about them, then.

(Fade.)

A lost teddy bear influences Veronica in more ways than one.

The Teddy Bear

The Teddy Bear was first presented at
The Pump House Theatre,
Watford

on 22 March 2015
with the following cast:

Veronica ... **Barbara Towell**

Veronica – *A woman in her fifties.*

(Lights Up. VERONICA stands, stares ahead.
Pause.
She addresses audience.)

VERONICA: The teddy bear had been in the shop window for a week.

I had pestered my mum about it every day.

'Too much money,' she said.

It really *was* special. It had sky blue eyes and a cherry red nose.

But what made it different were its gold-rimmed glasses.

I'd never seen a teddy with glasses before.

My dad said, 'The glasses are just for show.

The teddy doesn't need to wear glasses at all.

He's just a poser. A poser, that's all.

A bit of a show-off. That's all he is.

Are you *sure* you want him?'

'I'm sure! I'm sure!'

'But look at that hat!'

Yes, the teddy had a hat. A small beige trilby.

'It's ridiculous! *Look!*'

In those days, not many teddies wore hats.

'*Another* affectation,' sighed dad.

Mum poo-poohed him, too. He was too pretentious.

He wasn't their idea of a teddy at all.

Whoever heard of a teddy with a trilby?

'But he's different!' I pleaded.

'He's not very cuddly. He's the *least* cuddly teddy
I've ever seen,' said mum.

'And he's cross-eyed,' said dad.

'If you look closely at him, you'll see he's cross-
eyed.'

'He's not! He's not!'

It was clear to me, now, they didn't want to buy
him.

It's true, he was very pricey indeed.

But finally, dad said, 'Maybe next week. When I get
paid next week, we *might* buy him, then.'

(Pause.)

Well, next Friday came and dad was late home.

Always later on Fridays, he would come home at
eight.

Two hours later than other days. Every Friday was
the same.

He'd stop off with his mates for drinks after work.

(Pause.)

Mum let me stay up. It got way past my bedtime.

We waited and waited. Still no sign of dad.

'He *will* bring teddy, won't he?'

'Of course he will.'

'Are you sure?'

'He's already bought him,' she said. 'Dad phoned

me at lunchtime to tell me he'd bought him.'

'Wow! That's terrific!'

'You'll see teddy tomorrow. Be a good girl, eh?
Go to bed, now?'

(Pause.)

So I did go to bed, but found I couldn't sleep.

It took me ages to get off to sleep.

I was woken by angry shouting from downstairs.

The walls were wafer-thin. I could hear every word.

'What do you mean? You've left him on the bus?!

What the hell are we going to tell her now, eh?

I've told her you're bringing him home tonight,
right?'

'Look, I'm sorry. I'm sorry. I just fell asleep, woke
up at my stop and dashed off the bus ...'

'Without him? Terrific!'

'He'll turn up, I'm sure. I'll phone lost property, first
thing, alright?'

'And you're drunk again, aren't you?'

'Give me a break ... it was John's leaving party. The
whole thing dragged on ...

If we don't find the teddy, I'll buy another.

Just buy another. Not the end of the world.

Look, he's not unique, is he? He's not ... unique?

Anybody would think I'd lost the crown jewels!'
(Pause.)

The next day, I said nothing. Just kept very quiet.

Pretended I didn't know teddy was lost.

'Change of plan,' said mum. 'Dad will bring him home today. Something happened. He couldn't bring teddy home last night.'

'Will it be the same teddy? The one in the window?'

'Of course it will. 'Course it will.'

(Pause.)

But it wasn't the same teddy. My teddy *was* lost.

This new teddy was bland like a thousand others.

He had a stupid half-smile on his face and hardly any chin. A chinless wonder! And his clothes were so boring. No flair or panache.

'You'll get used to him.'

'Can't I have the other teddy, mum?'

'I'm afraid he's been sold, love. Sold to ... Japan.'

'To Japan?'

'A Japanese lady bought him.

There were only two made and she bought them both.

An old man made the teddies ... just as a hobby.

But he only made two, then the poor man died.'

'I don't like this new teddy.'

'He has *such* a nice smile ... Now come on now, Missy.

Be grateful,' said dad.

'Other girls have *no* teddies. Have no toys at all.'

'And he sings,' said mum. You've not heard him sing yet. A *singing* teddy. How about that"

Sure enough, he *did* sing. *The Teddy Bears Picnic.*
Over and over and over again.
'He's a nice voice, hasn't he? A very nice voice.
Not every teddy can sing like that.'
(Pause.)
Not many teddies would *want* to sing like that.
And *when* he sang, he looked so smug.
Oh, he fancied himself, big time, as a singer.
He really thought he was the bee's knees.
(Pause.)
But after two days, his voice started to crackle.
Just started to ... well ... stop and start. Break up.
It was almost as if he had a sore throat.
I almost ... *almost* felt sorry for him.
Things went downhill fast.
He lost all sense of rhythm.
On the third day he sounded like nothing on earth.
Of course, I pretended to be very upset.
Started sobbing in my bedroom, knowing they'd
hear.
'What's the matter?
What on earth's the matter?' they asked.
(Imitates child crying.) 'My teddy can't sing!
Can't sing anymore!'
Oh yes, I had *them* nearly crying as well.
A fine performance. A turning point. Yes.
Looking back, my first step to becoming an actress.

A pivotal point in me choosing a career.

'I'm taking him back!' dad was very annoyed.

'Tomorrow he's going back to the shop!

He was *very* expensive. And how does he sing?

Like a constipated Bing Crosby!'

(Pause.)

Mum told me, years later, she thought losing 'first' teddy made dad feel so guilty, he'd cut back on drink. She claimed he *never* came home drunk again.

(Remembering.) The thing is, some nights he didn't come home at all ... Even so, she convinced herself losing teddy had helped save her marriage.

Well, something like that.

This sounded to me like a load of old rubbish.

Dad continued drinking beer out of his ears. Still, they both seemed happy. Well, most of the time.

Like most couples, they had lots of ups and downs.

But they *did* love each other. I'm certain of that.

They stayed together through thick and through thin.

(Pause.)

I persuaded them both I didn't want any more teddies. They ended up buying a dolls' house instead. I played with this for hours on end.

Later on, I played Nora in Ibsen's Dolls' House.

(Pause.)

But sometimes I still dream of Teddy, wondering if he's still out there, living in Japan.

In one of my dreams, he's *here.* I've found him.

Not in Japan. But in a charity shop.

(Pause.)

In this dream, he has a very bleary eye.

I'm afraid the years have not been kind.

He's got a wonky leg and a very dodgy arm.

His trilby's very battered. Quite dirty as well.

And his gold-rimmed glasses are lopsided, now.

The nose-piece is held together with tape!

But he still wears the trilby at a very rakish angle
and he still has a mischievous twinkle in his eye.

He still looks like a slightly eccentric Professor.

(Thoughtful, reflects.) A bit like my husband, really.

(Fade.)

Will Frank receive a fond farewell?

Farewell To Frank

Farewell To Frank was first presented at
The Harrow Arts Centre

on 7 January 2016
with the following cast:

Eva ... **Julia Underwood**

Eva – *A woman in her late fifties.*

(Lights up. EVA is sitting at a table, drinking wine.
She is slightly tipsy.
She addresses a framed photograph on the table.
Pause.)

EVA: What amazes me is you didn't think I knew.
You were both convinced I knew nothing at all.
It was laughable, really. Looking back.
Discretion? An alien concept to *her*.
I'm surprised she just didn't leave her knickers in our bed.
It was all so obvious. Right from the start.
(Pause.)
(She gulps some wine.)
It's been three months, now, since you ... passed away.
I've still not decided what to do.
About this place, I mean. About this house.
On the one hand, it's too big for just one person.
Sometimes I just feel lost in the space.
Other times, the space gives me ... *(Shrugs.)* a kind of comfort.
Comfort? Come off it. That's *hardly* the word.
Even so, we both lived here thirty-six years.
That's a very long time in anyone's book.

The idea of moving to a smaller place *now* ... no, forget it. Complete non starter.

(Pause.)

What I really can't stand is all the *sympathy*.

Oh, people mean well. I know they mean well.

But it's just ... well, it's all just so ... unrelenting.

'How are you *coping?* How *are* you, now?

If you feel a bit lonely, why not pop round?

Have you thought of joining The New Women's Guild?

And what about Yoga? Pilates? Tai Chi'?

Someone even suggested I should start playing Whist.

(Pause.)

What's it like where you are? Wherever you are?

Are you looking down at me? Having a laugh?

Sometimes I have this vision of you looking so smug.

You're just sitting up there on a kind of chaise longue.

I can see you quite clearly. You're smoking your pipe.

Now you're dead, you can smoke it as much as you like.

No more lectures from me on how it's ruining your health.

You're just puffing away. Not a care in the world.

(Pause.)

When I'm out in the garden, I keep hearing your voice.

Yesterday I was hearing your voice all the time.

(Imitates Frank's north country accent.)

'Mind how you go with the Magnolia tree.

Don't prune it too much. Don't take too much off.

And remember the Hollyhocks and Azaleas.

Water them both at least twice a week through the Spring, and *do* keep an eye on the lawn.'

I found myself saying, *'Yes dear. Yes, I will.'*

(Pause.)

The vicar popped in to see me yesterday.

He's certain you're now in the arms of God.

I found myself wishing *I* felt so certain.

Must be marvellous feeling as certain as that.

(Pause.)

I didn't mention you were a non believer.

I thought that might muddy the waters too much.

He still thinks you were always *forced* to work Sundays.

Let's let him carry on thinking that, eh?

(Pause.)

Well, anyway, he wants me to become a Church Member.

(Imitates vicar's plumy voice.)

'You've been on the fringes of the church for too long.

We would be *delighted* to welcome you in.

For the church to be *alive* we need new ideas.

For instance, we're now thinking *flexible seating.*

We're thinking of ripping out all of the pews.

Pews are old hat. Outdated. Completely divisive.

The vicar in his pulpit? Far too remote!

He needs to be closer to his congregation.

To communicate as a neighbour and friend.

To reach out more. Show people what he's got to share.'

('Shocked'.) At this point I noticed his fly was half undone!

Men *are* careless sometimes. Forget to zip up.

I'm sure it *was* that. Just carelessness. Yes.

When all's said and done, he's a vicar after all.

(Nods, although not entirely convinced.)

Just sheer absentmindedness. That's all it was.

(Pause.)

Some men are sloppy dressers.

I'm not getting *too* excited. *(Small chuckle.)*

I don't *think* I've become an object of desire ... but if I were a dolly bird, I wouldn't mind betting he'd show some respect, then? Take more care?

(Pause.)

Well, he'd no sooner gone, then who should turn up Elaine Smethwick. An old school friend.

I don't think you ever met her.

I haven't seen her for a while.

It turned out she'd lost her husband as well.

Nearly two years ago. He jumped off a cliff.

By the time she'd finished telling me how lonely life can be without your partner, how long the nights are, how you never really get over it at all ... I felt like jumping off a cliff too.

(Pause.)

(Picks up framed photograph.)

This is *still* my favourite photograph of us.

When we were young. Before you lost your hair.

Having said that, you always quite suited baldness.

You carried it off with a certain panache.

But when you were young, you had such nice hair.

(Pause.)

Such wavy hair.

(Pause.)

Yesterday I took a book out of the library.

A book of cartoons. *Sex for geriatrics.*

I thought it might make me laugh a bit and it did.

There was one with an old man and woman in bed.

The bedclothes are bulging up on the man's side.

His wife's looking anxious, so he tries to reassure her.

(Imitates old man's voice.)

'Don't worry, my dear. There's no need to worry.

It's only ... *(Starts to giggle)* rigour mortis'!

(She giggles, starts to laugh.

The laughter stops.

She gulps wine, stares ahead.

Pause.)

There was no trace of rigour mortis with you, but for quite a long time *you* couldn't manage it too.

Then the blue pill had no sooner come to your rescue and *my* trouble started. What can you say?

(Pause.)

I *did* understand. Understood all too well.

Things were never the same in that department since my operation. *Look,* the thing was … if you'd been more discreet, I might have just … well … what the eye doesn't see, the heart doesn't grieve?

(Pause.)

I knew you still loved me. You only loved *me.*

With her, it was only sex after all.

But you didn't have to lie to me.

Getting her to ring me? Your *wonderful* secretary ringing all the time?

(Imitates secretary's brisk, slightly offhand voice.)

'Frank asked me to ring you. He has to work late.

He told me to tell you not to wait up.'

(Pause.)

Oh, I understood. A woman half your age?

A great boost to your ego. Of course she was.

But you shouldn't have been taking the blue pill at all.

Okay, true enough, it's helped thousands of men

but in *your* case you *knew* it was ... well ... *a big risk.*

(Angrily.) You'd a heart condition, you bloody fool!

(Pause.)

Must have been a shock for her. Terrible shock.

I *do* hope they didn't have to prise you off.

You never *did* manage to lose any weight.

Too many fresh cream cakes and Walnut Whips.

(Pause.)

(Raises glass to toast.) Well, here's to you anyway.

Wherever you are. To the good times we had.

To all our *good* times.

Keep your pecker up, won't you?

On second thoughts, *don't.*

Rest in peace now, Frank.

Rest in peace.

(She drains her glass.

Fade.)

'They've put me in a ward with a load of
old women.
What annoys me is they think I'm old.'

Waiting For Tea

Waiting For Tea was first presented by
Tin Shed Theatre Company at

The Davenham Players Theatre,
Davenham, Northwich

On 28 April 2011
with the following cast:

Mary ... **Margaret Smith**

Mary – *A woman of eighty-three.*

(Lights up. A hospital ward. MARY stands with a Zimmer Frame.)

MARY: They've put me in a ward with a load of old women.

What annoys me is they think *I'm old.*

And I'm not. I'm not old. I'm not old at all.

In my head, I'm still young. *(Taps head.)* I'm still young in here.

Okay, I know some days are better than others.

There's good days and bad days. I don't dispute that but the point is *(Taps forehead.)* up here, I'm as sound as a bell.

I'm as sharp as a razor. Why can't they see that?

Why can't they just see I'm not old inside?

(Pause.)

They don't try and see.

(Pause.)

Bear in mind, though, the nurses have a lot to put up with.

Some of the patients in here, they're ... well ... there's one or two here ... well, they shouldn't be in here. They should be *somewhere else,* if you know what I mean? *(Points.)* Take Betty over there.

Nutty as a fruitcake. She excelled herself last night, make no mistake.

She got up in the night. The middle of the night.

Goes to each bedside table ... collecting false teeth.

When she's finished, she dumps them all in a sink at the end of the ward.

Imagine! Well. This was last night. They've still not sorted it out.

They still don't know which teeth are which.

(Points to left.) Some of the women say *none* of them are theirs.

(Pause.)

God, what a mess.

(Pause.)

(Leans forward, secretively confides.) Of course, I always make a point of sleeping in mine. You can't be too careful in places like this. It's important to stay ahead of the game.

Otherwise, like *them,* I'd have lost my teeth too.

(Pause.)

(Small chuckle.) I shouldn't laugh, I know. I know I shouldn't laugh, but ... talk about putting your foot in it?

Well ... you see Ethel over there? She was sitting there, glum, when her son came to visit her this afternoon.

Of course, he had no idea of what had happened with the teeth and the first thing he said was, 'Come on, Mum. Cheer up.

Cheer up. Stop looking so down in the mouth!

You look ... *(Giggles, despite herself)* absolutely sick to the teeth!'

What's wrong'? Well, I very nearly wet myself.

I couldn't stop laughing. They thought I'd gone mad.

The nurse had to wheel me out of the ward.

(Shakes head, wipes away tears of laughter.)

Dear oh dear oh dear.

(Pause.)

(Looks at watch.) Oh she is late today. She's getting worse.

She's supposed to bring the tea round at three.

I *do* wish she'd come. I'm spitting feathers.

(Pause.)

It's quarter to four.

(Pause.)

At least it's warm in here. Always nice and warm.

Not like my flat. That can get a bit cold.

Still, even so, I'll be glad to get back.

(Pause.)

Back to my flat.

(Pause.)

My son's coming tonight. He's a bit of a writer.

He tries to get me writing as well.

Nothing much. Just one or two poems here and there.

He said, 'Mum, writing poems is therapeutic. Instead of moaning about how cold it is, why don't you try writing a poem about it?'

(Pause.)

So that's what I did.

(Pause.)

It's a little bit short. Well, it is ... short, but my son says all good poetry is *condensed.* He said all good poetry is *pared down. Compressed.*

Are you ready, then? Here it is.

(Pause.)

(She clears her throat, composes herself, starts to read in a more modulated, slightly affected voice.)

If you are cold and three weeks old ... lay down and bloody die.

(Pause.)

(Own voice again.) That's all I could write about being cold.

I'd much rather write a poem about sex.

Trouble is, I've almost forgotten what it's like.

(Quickly points, emphatic.) Now, I did say *almost.*

Don't write me off yet.

(Leans forward, secretively confides.) Between you and me, there's this man who works in the hospital canteen.

He's got the hots for me. *Yes.* Oh, he fancies me rotten.

It stands out a mile. He always gives me a bigger dessert.

You know, extra fruit pudding and double whipped cream.

Men are so transparent, I always think. Yes.

There's this window cleaner too. Comes here once a

week.

He's always lingering. Chatting me up.

(Points.) This window by my bed ... he cleans it *twice.*

So painfully obvious. Y'know what I mean?

Even so, the thing is, when I'm back on my feet, I might give them both a bit of a whirl.

If they play their cards right ... well, who knows?

Like they say, you're a long time dead.

(Pause.)

Reg wouldn't ... wouldn't mind.

I know he wouldn't mind. Didn't he tell me?

He said, 'Just don't sit around moping.

When I'm dead, get out there and find someone else.

Just find a replacement. Find someone else.'

(Pauses, reflects, then speaks softly.)

Well, there *is* no replacement, you bloody fool.

Why did you have to go first?

(Pause.)

They warned you, didn't they? Time and again, they told you to quit the fags and the booze.

But no, you wouldn't listen. You never would listen.

(Impatiently.) So don't come crying to me.

(Pause.)

What am I saying? Don't come crying to me?

How could you come crying? You're supposed to be dead.

(Softer.) But it's ten years, now. Do you realise that?

And I still see you standing ... at the side of the bed.

Every morning I wake up, I still hear your voice.

'I've brought you a nice cup of tea.'

(Pause.)

(She silently sobs, quickly recovers, wipes eyes, straightens, stares resolutely ahead.)

(Pause.)

My son doesn't think I'll get back on my feet.

He's a real ray of sunshine, my son. Oh yes.

He says, 'Let's face it, Mum.' *He's* facing nothing.

I'm the one facing it, not him. Right?

He keeps saying, 'Let's face it, you won't walk again. They've as good as told you, you won't walk again.'

Well, I know what he wants. It's as clear as day.

He wants me to sell up, go live in a home.

He keeps saying, *(Imitates son's whining voice.)* 'Mum, you need around the clock care.'

(Exasperated.) Where *is* she with that tea?

(Pause.)

(Softer.) They haven't ... *said* I won't walk again. What they've said is my knee and hip joints are bad.

Full of Arthritis. Rheumatoid Arthritis.

(Pause.)

They haven't ... said.

(Pause.)

(Shrugs.) So I fell down the stairs and I'm badly bruised.

It's shaken me up. No doubt about that.

But there's nothing broken. There's no bones broken.

(Pause.)

I'm still in one piece.

(Pause.)

All I'm looking to do is just get to that toilet.

(Small chuckle.) No, not this minute, if you know what I mean, but in ... the future ... after two or three weeks ... with the Zimmer Frame ... just ... just walk there myself.

By myself ... then I'll know ... I'll be ready... for home.

(Pause.)

I'll know I can cope.

(Pause.)

My son took me once to a play by someone ... there were two old people in dustbins. Well ... to be honest, I've had more fun at the dentist. God in heaven! Real bundle of laughs.

I've got news for *that* writer. I'm not in a dustbin.

I've still got some spirit. I'm not in one yet.

I'm not in a dustbin and *never will be.*

Put *that* in your pipe, Sonny Jim!

(Pause.)

(She stands with the Zimmer, moves one small step, then another.)

(Fade.)

STANDING ALONE

'The silence was there. It was always there. Almost comforting, then. Comforting? No...'

The Silence

The Silence was first presented by
Tin Shed Theatre Company at
The Davenham Players Theatre,
Davenham, Northwich

on 28 April 2011
with the following cast:

Gem ... **Sue Tamlin**

Gem – *A woman in her early fifties.*

(House lights to blackout. Lights snap on.
A dead man dangles by the neck from a rope
suspended from a beam.
Silence.
GEM appears.
She stands a moment, stares at the body.
Silence.)

GEM: I phoned them. They're coming. They'll soon be here now.

The policeman I spoke to seemed ... so calm.

I expect they're used to it. Cases like this.

(Pause.)

They'll soon be here now.

(Pause.)

I refuse to feel guilty. You did it yourself. No one else is to blame.

No one else. Just you. It was your decision. You did it yourself.

(Pause.)

You hanged yourself.

(Pause.)

We should have finished it ... years ago.

Realised what ... what the situation was.

There was nothing left. Nothing. What was the point?

(Pause.)

What was the point?

(Pause.)

(Soft.) Can't tell me now, can you? Where are you now?

Heaven? Hell? Or nowhere at all? My guess is nowhere.

Still ... who knows?

(Pause.)

Nobody knows.

(Pause.)

It's funny, I never *did* like that beam. I was never sure of it.

Right from the start. 'Let's make it more *Olde Worlde*,' you said.

'More traditional. More cosy. Let's make it more quaint.

Yes, let's knock the wall down. Have a nice beam.'

(Pause.)

Have a nice beam.

(Pause.)

Why'd you pick today anyway? Glorious morning. Sun shining away.

Not a cloud in the sky. I'd have thought you'd have waited until it was dull. Waited until it rained. No?

I'd have thought rain was more conducive. I mean, well, when the sun's shining ... must be more ... still, I suppose when you've made your mind up, that's it.

73

(Pause.)

Rain or shine.

(Pause.)

It rained when I met you. Torrential. Remember? The bus was late?

I'd been waiting an hour. Well, a long time anyway. Started to rain.

You stopped your car. Gave me a lift.

(Pause.)

(Emphatic.) It *wasn't* just that he was younger than you.

He wasn't much younger. Five years or so. It was attitude. Outlook.

He made me laugh. He was funny. Amusing.

He treated me ... well ... as a person. *A person.* He made me smile.

(Pause.)

He made me laugh.

(Pause.)

You made me laugh once. When we were young.

You always made me laugh a lot then.

I mean, we had our good times, didn't we?

Mmm? We had our moments. Too bloody true.

(Small chuckle.) That day at the fair. I'll never forget it. Laugh?

The bloody ghost train broke down. We were stuck in a tunnel.

Bats and skeletons touching me up ... as well as

you.

You were terrible then. Couldn't keep you off. Couldn't believe it.

Of all the places to pick! You've never been half as inventive since.

Of all the places to choose ...

(Silence.)

Perhaps if we'd had a child, we might ... a little boy ... we might have been ... well ... who knows? Happier? More fulfilled?

I always wanted a child.

(Pause.)

You wanted one too. I'm sorry I couldn't but that was our lot.

I mean, what can you do? It's different today. There's fertility drugs.

There was nothing like that then. Still, *he* has two children.

Both grown up. Never sees them. Never. They're strangers. Remote.

One thing's for certain, *they* didn't stop the rot.

They didn't stop *his* marriage hitting the rocks.

If a marriage is over, kids or no kids, it's over. Finished. Kaput.

(Pause.)

(Soft.) I won't see him again. It finished last week.

He's found someone younger. Disappeared. Gone.

I tried to tell you last night. Just couldn't ... couldn't speak.

(Pause.)

Couldn't get it out.

(Pause.)

(Suddenly aggressive.) You changed. Grew older. We all grow older, it's true, but you grew older *inside*. Something died inside you.

You aged inside.

(Pause.)

Something died.

(Pause.)

(Softer.) We couldn't ... couldn't talk. The silence ... spread.

Spread out like a cloak. I couldn't ... couldn't breathe ... couldn't breathe ... suffocating ... had to have air.

(Pause.)

Had to have sun.

(Pause.)

I turned. He was there. He offered me change. From sameness.

Drabness. Routine. Grind. The whole worn out caboodle.

He offered me hope.

(Pause.)

He offered me *life*.

(Pause.)

We were happy at first. In the early days. Yes? We were happy.

Contented. No need for words. The silence was there.

It was always there. *(Small chuckle.)* Almost comforting then.

Comforting? No ... no, that's the wrong word. It was never *that*.

It was never comforting. Golden? No. It was there. Just there.

It didn't need to be filled. Just there. That's all. Nothing more.

No ... *(Recalling)* And sometimes it *was* golden.

Once we lay on a bank. By a stream. Near a bridge ... in Cornwall, I think. We lay in the sun. All day in the sun. You rubbing my back all over with oil. My shoulders ... back ... my bottom ... thighs ... your hands ... gently rubbing ... all over with oil ... no words ... hours on end ... no need for words ... no words ... silence ... silence ... sun. Halfway upstream a man was fishing.

I watched him. Silent. Casting his rod then sitting, still, waiting.

Crouched like a toad. Your fingers ... massaging ... soft ... firm ... firm, turning me over ... brown all over ... casting his line ... dark shape in the sun ... no cloud in the sky ... I love you you said ... love you I said love you too ...

(Fade.)

STANDING ALONE

A new three piece suite brings about changes for Ron.

Three Piece Suite

Three Piece Suite was first presented as part of
The Harrow Drama Festival
by Belmont Theatre Company
at The Travellers Theatre, Harrow

on 8 July 2003
with the following cast:

Ron ... **Jeff Clarke**

Ron – *A man in his forties.*

(Lights up. Country roadside.
RON sits on a rock, a cigarette packet next to him.
He holds an unlit cigarette and lighter.
He is stripped down to underpants and socks.
He stands, stares ahead.
Silence.)

RON: My wife, Ann, said we needed to make more money.

We need new furniture. That's what she said. A new three piece suite.

True enough, she was right. Our old suite was in a bit of a state.

Well and truly knackered. No doubt about that. The fabric was worn.

Gone threadbare. A mess. There were springs sticking out.

She said, 'Ron, I'm ashamed. Too ashamed to invite people round.'

(Pause.)

Then she had this idea. It *was* her idea.

'Why don't you try mini-cabbing?' She said.

'In the evenings,' she said. 'For a limited time. Just to get enough cash to buy a new suite?' Well, I gave it some thought.

I thought what can I lose? If it works out, I thought, I can do it full-time. My day job in the factory was pissing me off.

(Pause.)

So I gave it a go.

(Pause.)

I found I preferred it. Suited me well. Trips out to the airport ... bloody good tips. Beat working in a lousy factory by a mile.

(Pause.)

More than a mile.

(Pause.)

Not being hemmed in. I quite liked that. Not being hemmed in by four factory walls. My own boss as well ... no one breathing down my neck.

(Pause.)

I liked that too.

(Pause.)

Trouble was, by the time I'd made enough cash to put down a deposit, she'd changed her mind. She didn't want Draylon. Considered it naff.

Decided she wanted a leather suite instead. She'd seen one in a new shop opened down the road. This suite was expensive.

Eight hundred more. But I thought, what the hell, if it makes her happy ...

(Pause.)

If that's what it takes ...

(Pause.)

I gotta admit it wasn't *my* taste. Bright yellow, it was.

Too gaudy for me. But she said it would ... now, what was it she said?

She said it would *lift things. Lift ... the room.* I had visions of the room floating out of the house.

(Pause.)

Lift the room.

(Pause.)

Still, the thing was, *she* liked it. Right? I mean, that was the main thing.

She liked the suite. If she likes it, I thought, she'll stop moaning on.

(Pause.)

And then it arrived.

(Pause.)

I got home one evening and there it was. Pride of place. Right there.

Right there in the room. She was over the moon. And it *did* look good.

It looked the business. Much better than I thought.

Well, we stood and admired it. Then we sat down.

(Pause.)

Then we *lay* down.

(Pause.)

'Let's christen it,' she said. 'The sofa,' she said.

It had been so long ... I thought that side was dead. I thought that side was finished. Over and done.

(Pause.)

Finished for good.

(Pause.)

(Softer.) Couldn't believe it, the way she made love to me then.

Like when we were young. Like when we first wed.

She made me feel ... wanted. Wanted again.
(Pause.)

First time in years.

(Pause.)

Afterwards, we just fell asleep. Fell asleep for a while in each others arms. When we woke, she noticed the stitching on the arm.

The stitching on the arm of the sofa had come loose.

A small detail, but ... well it *was* a new suite.

So anyway, I rang the manager of the shop.

He promised to send someone round the next day.

The next day no one came. I got on to him again.

He apologised. Said the repair man was ill.

Said he'd fallen ill. Sudden. Gone down with the flu.

Said he'd send the man round when he came back to work.

Meanwhile, he was sorry. Could we just wait a while?

(Pause.)

That's what we did.

(Pause.)

We waited two weeks. In that whole two weeks, my wife couldn't take her eyes off this stitching on the arm. It became ... an obsession.

No exaggeration. She convinced herself it was just getting worse.

Then after four weeks the repair man came.

I got home from work and the job had been done. He'd re-stitched it.

Perfect. The wife was well pleased.

(Pause.)

Then she found something else.

(Pause.)

From this point on she kept finding things wrong.

It seemed the repair man was never away. First of all, the stitching.

Then the leather on the seats. Then the innards on the seats ... and the springing on the chair. Then a castor came off.

He came round to fix that.

(Pause.)

He was never away.

(Pause.)

Then one day I came home early from work. I was feeling ropey.

Just feeling quite ill. So I came home early to get my head down.

(Pause.)

He was there then, too.

(Pause.)

He just got up and dressed. She got up and

dressed. We said nothing.

None of us. Nobody spoke. Then he left. I slashed the suite up with a knife. She went to live with her sister.

(Pause.)

I carried on mini-cabbing. Full-time.

(Pause.)

That is, 'til tonight.

(Pause.)

At least they didn't take everything. Driving off in my car with my clothes and my takings, they threw out my fags.

(Small chuckle.) That was nice of them, anyway. Don't you think?

At least they left me a smoke?

(Pause.)

I'll get a lift soon. What is it they say? You gotta get lucky sometime?

(Pause.)

Trouble is ... this road ... there's not many cars ...

(Pause.)

Not sure where I am ...

(He thumbs an approaching car.)

(Fade.)

STANDING ALONE

'Some people are just ... just too far away.'

Whilst Feeding The Cats

Whilst Feeding The Cats was first presented by
East Lane Theatre Company at
East Lane Theatre, Wembley, London

on 23 August 2015
with the following cast:

Malcolm ... **Melville Lovatt**

Malcolm – *A man in his mid sixties.*

*(Lights up. MALCOLM stands, stares ahead.
Pause. He refers to audience.)*

MALCOLM: When I left school at fifteen, my very
first job was working as a clerk in a corn
merchant's mill.

I was interviewed by the foreman, Mr Jordan.

Miss Winder, the owner's daughter sat in.

She was very well spoken. Quite aristocratic.

Well, she seemed aristocratic to a boy like me.

*(Imitates Mr Jordan's voice with a pronounced
northern accent.)*

'We'll take you on a month's trial,' Mr Jordan said.

'I might add, there's been lots of lads after this job.

I must have interviewed a dozen last week.

Jobs are scarce, right now. No doubt about that.

So it's three pounds to start, then. After a month, if
we're happy, it rises to three pounds ten. Three
pounds, ten shillings. Plus free cups of tea. We
might even throw in a biscuit or two.'

(Pause.)

Seems like yesterday, sometimes.

Nineteen sixty-two in a small northern provincial
town.

The mill was ancient. Falling to pieces.

Dickensian? *(Small chuckle.)* Well, that was hardly

the word.

I used to sit on a very high stool. Recording all the deliveries of corn.

This part wasn't too bad. Sitting on the stool.

No, the worst part was having to feed all the cats.

Used to dread it, I did. Every day at three o'clock, Mr Jordan would announce, 'It's time to feed the cats.'

Then I'd set off walking the length of the mill to where all the cat food was stored, the far end.

There were so many cats there. Twenty three!

Small wonder we never saw any mice.

I felt like the pied piper. The cats saw me coming and followed me all the way to their food.

(Pause.)

This went on for two weeks.

I usually stood and watched them eating and drinking their milk. This took quite a while.

One day I got bored. Left them to it and went for a stroll around the mill.

(Pause.)

There were parts of this mill which were *very* old.

Dating back to eighteen twenty or so.

There were rooms, the far end, which were no longer used. Where the floorboards were rotting. Considered unsafe. There was no need to go in these rooms at all.

(Shrugs.) The thing was, I was bored. I was just … just bored.

(Pause.)

Well, the next thing was, I opened the door to one of the rooms and looked inside.

There was nothing there. Nothing. Completely empty.

I moved to a second room, opened the door, expecting to find this room pretty much the same.

(Pause.)

It wasn't the same.

(Pause.)

This room was in much better condition.

It was obvious the room had been cared for more.

There was even an old chaise longue and a chair.

And a couple of paintings. Old paintings on the walls.

(Pause.)

As I stood there, pondering, I heard faint noises.

Faint ... faint noises. Sounded like groans.

The room was L-shaped, I forgot to mention.

The noises were coming from where I couldn't see.

Well, I didn't hang around.

Got out of there, sharpish. *(Small chuckle.)*

Decided to call it a day.

(Pause.)

Looking back, I *should* have just left it at that.

It was none of my business, anyway. Right?

Should have just walked away.

I don't know why I didn't. Idle curiosity?

Call it what you like.

All I know is, just leaving it didn't seem an option.

The thing was, that night, I found I couldn't sleep.

I kept hearing those noises. All through the night.

(Pause.)

They just wouldn't go away.

(Pause.)

Three o'clock the next day. 'Time to feed the cats.'

I set off walking the length of the mill.

This time was different. The cats didn't come out to follow me like they always had before.

But I found them there, waiting. All lying there, waiting.

Just waiting for me to open their tins.

(Pause.)

I opened their tins, and then left them to it.

Wandered back, again, to the L-shaped room.

I stood, listening. Silence. No noises at all.

I decided, this time, I'd just take a look in.

I just peered around the corner, and there they were!

Mr Jordan and Miss Winder, sitting up in bed!

They were both sitting up in a four poster bed, with fancy cups and saucers, drinking tea!

They didn't see me. I ducked back around the corner.

Stood there a few moments, rooted to the spot.

Then I just crept away. Just crept back to the cats.

I was *certain* I hadn't been spotted.

(Pause.)

The next day Mr Jordan called me into his office.

I thought, *This is it.* They *did* see me after all.

And my month's trial's finished. He'll be giving me the boot.

'Sit down,' he said. 'Tea? Have a biscuit.'

(Pause.)

'Well, to cut to the chase, we're *reasonably* happy.

Reasonably happy with you,' he said.

'I've spoken to the owner, Mr Winder.

'Mr Winder has asked me to increase your wage.

But there's no room for slacking.

I'm away on business to Blackpool tomorrow.

I'm away a few days. Whilst I'm gone, Miss Winder is in charge of the office. I expect you to give her your full support.'

(Pause.)

With Mr Jordan gone, things went on the same.

Except now, Miss Winder said, 'Time to feed the cats.'

I fed them at three o'clock every day.

Things just ticked over, pretty much as before.

Until one day, I was feeling knackered.

I decided I'd just skive off for a bit.

I left the cats, eating. Walked over to the room.

Crashed out. Fell asleep on the four poster bed.

God knows how long I slept for. Went out like a light.

When I woke, it was late. It was time to go home.

Miss Winder was in shadow. Standing by the bed.

I expected to just be sacked on the spot.

Instead, she said nothing. Said nothing at all.

Just lay down beside me. On top of the bed.

She'd been crying, I think. Her eyes were quite red.

(Pause.)

We lay quite still.

(Pause.)

'Just hold me,' she said. 'Just hold me.'

I did. Just held her. I didn't ... didn't know what to say.

We just lay there, in silence, for what seemed like an hour.

Then she turned to me. Looked at me. Kissed me.

(Pause.)

There's a line in a song. A Bobby Goldsboro song.

I will chase the boy in you away.

Well, you'd better believe it. That's what she did.

She well and truly chased the boy in me away.

(Pause.)

I was only fifteen. No experience at all.

No experience at all of love or sex.

By the time we'd finished, I was several jumps

ahead.

I've never met anyone like her again.

(Pause.)

Afterwards, she handed me a letter.

Told me she had to go away the next day.

She handed me the letter to give to Mr Jordan.

(Pause.)

The next day she was gone.

(Pause.)

It only happened once. I never saw her again.

'She's gone off to London to study,' they said.

I heard a rumour she'd gone for an abortion.

Who knows what the truth was? Who ... who knows?

(Pause.)

Mr Jordan didn't seem like the same man at all.

From then on, his mind seemed to be somewhere else.

I left. Packed the job in, pretty soon after.

Just before I left, Mr Jordan got the sack.

(Pause.)

Looking back, I suppose he *was* pushing his luck.

The boss's daughter? A lot younger than him?

From a different class, too. A different ... well ...

maybe class counted a bit more than now?

(Pause.)

A few weeks later, I read in the paper, they'd found

Mr Jordan hanging from a tree.

Some woman was walking her dog in the park.

And there he was. I mean, what can you say?

(Pause.)

Sure enough I could see he was falling apart.

But what could *I* say to him? What could *I* do?

I had no idea what was in the letter.

Some people are just ... just too far away.

(Pause.)

Britain changed soon after. *Very* soon after.

The music scene was beginning to explode.

The Beatles. The Stones. The Swinging Blue Jeans.

The Who. The Animals. The Hollies. The Kinks.

'The times, they are a changin', wailed Dylan.

Later on, people wore flowers in their hair.

Free love became the order of the day.

All in the blink of an eye.

(Fade.)

STANDING ALONE

'It was no great mystery. I couldn't find the key. Had no reason to go in the bloody shed at all!'

The Retirement Plan

The Retirement Plan was first presented by
East Lane Theatre Company at
East Lane Theatre, Wembley, London

on 23 August 2015
with the following cast:

Owen ... **Barry Serjent**

Owen – *A man in his sixties.*

(Lights up. OWEN sits at a small kitchen table. He is drinking whisky.
(Pause.)

OWEN: People joke about this sort of thing all the time.

But nobody thinks it will happen to them.

I mean, what are the odds? A thousand to one?

(Pause.)

I'd say more than that.

(Pause.)

(He gulps whisky, drains glass, stares ahead.)

I had mixed feelings about retirement.

On the one hand, I couldn't wait to give up my job.

I was fed up with travelling week after week.

I worked as a rep, you see. Travelled *a lot.*

On the other hand, I sometimes found myself wondering, how long would it take for us both to … adjust?

The financial side of it wasn't an issue. We had enough cash.

No, the only thing was … it was just we weren't used to being together for seven days a week. My work took me away.

I joined Jan at the weekends, most of the time.

This arrangement had gone on year after year.

But I wouldn't want you thinking we weren't ... close.

We'd been married thirty odd years, after all.

We just didn't see the need for continual contact.

But our marriage was solid. Solid as a rock.

For retirement, we decided to stick to our plan.

Our *shorter term* retirement plan.

First, we'd sell our house and move to a bungalow.

We'd buy something special on the south coast.

And then we'd do cruises. Go on lots of cruises.

Later on we would visit our daughter in The States.

(He takes out a cigarette, changes his mind, puts cigarette back into packet.)

When Jan first saw this house, she was over the moon.

Well I should say *we. We* were over the moon.

We'd been looking at bungalows for nearly a year.

Okay, we were picky, but it wasn't *just* that.

All the places we looked at were ... how shall I say?

Too small? Too large? Too far out in the sticks?

We were just on the verge of calling it a day.

Then, well ... well, *this* house turned up.

(Pause.)

It was just what we wanted for our retirement.

A bungalow which didn't need any work.

All the work had been done by the property developer.

New kitchen. New bathroom. Subdued ceiling lights.

The décor, has it happened, was just to our taste.

The location was perfect. The price was just right.

But what *really* sold it to us was the garden.

The garden was really more like a small park.

We were both keen gardeners. Well, I still am.

It suited us both to a tee.

(Pause.)

That first summer was perfect. Jan loved the garden.

Yes, she was out there every single day.

Planting flowers. Planting shrubs. Trimming all the hedges.

She even created a vegetable patch.

She was happy as Larry. I couldn't wait to join her.

I had fifteen months to go before *I* retired.

But I joined her at weekends. We were out there together in the garden most weekends. Golden days.

(Pause.)

I should explain, we had *two* garden sheds.

One fairly new. And one very old.

The old one was really falling to bits.

Half hidden behind bushes. It was at the far end.

The developer had left it. I had no call to use it.

Jan wanted to knock it down right from the start.

'It's an eyesore,' she said. Well, of course, she was

right.

'Neither use nor ornament.' I couldn't agree more.

We found it was locked. Hadn't been used for years.

I couldn't find a key to it. Searched high and low.

To keep Jan happy, I agreed to do it.

Said I'd knock it down the following month.

(Pause.)

Looking back, I suppose I *did* drag my heels.

I admit I just kept on putting it off.

The bottom line was *it didn't seem important.*

At any rate, it didn't seem important to *me.*

When all's said and done, it was hidden behind bushes.

You could hardly see the damned thing at all.

(Pause.)

'When are you going to knock it down, Owen'?

It became Jan's obsession. She kept on and on.

She just kept on about it. Driving me nuts.

So, finally I got this small firm to do it.

I couldn't be bothered to do it myself.

I paid in advance and just left for work.

I expected the job done when I got back.

That's it, I thought. Sorted.

She'll stop moaning, now. She'll be happier, now.

End of story.

(He gulps whisky, draining glass, swiftly refills glass, stares ahead.)

(Pause.)

The police just turned up. No warning at all.

Turned up at my office, later in the day.

'We'd like you to accompany us back to your house.'

That was it. No details. That's all they said.

When we got to the house, it was all cordoned off.

They'd thrown a marquee up around the old shed.

Flashing lights. Sirens. It all seemed unreal.

Poor Jan was stressed out. As white as a sheet.

The police couldn't understand why the shed was locked.

Why we'd never looked in it, having lived here a year.

It was no great mystery. I couldn't find the key.

(Angrily.) Had no reason to go in the bloody shed at all!

I mean, more to the point, Why didn't *they* look in it when the guy was reported missing at the time?

WHY DIDN'T *THEY* PULL THEIR FINGERS OUT, *THEN?*

WHY THE HELL DIDN'T *THEY* DO A PROPER SEARCH, *THEN?!*

(He quickly gulps whisky, slams down glass.

He composes himself, speaks evenly.)

The skeleton had been in the shed for eight years.

It was wearing a dark suit, pink shirt and tie.

The key to the shed was in its pocket.

Along with a note. A suicide note.

(Indifferently.) I was told two men had once lived in the house.

It seems they were gay and argued like mad.

John Evans's *partner* had threatened to leave him.

Evans had gone missing soon after that.

(Pause.)

At the end of the day, I mean, what can you say?

Jan was never the same from that day on.

She wouldn't go in the garden, ever again.

And she hardly talked to me. Hardly talked.

It's true we had never done much talking.

Looking back, perhaps we should have talked more.

But she seemed ... just seemed to go into a shell.

She said she couldn't ... continue living in the house.

One day, she just turned to me. Turned to me.

Said, 'All we had was the garden. There's nothing else left'.

I said, 'How do you mean? There's nothing else left?'

'All we had was the garden,' was all she could say.

Well, I've never accepted that's all we had.

She *knows* that's rubbish. She's upset, that's all.

I mean, hang on a minute, she's forgetting something.

(Small chuckle.) We've been together for thirty odd years!

(Pause.)

She *will* get over it, make no mistake.

People get over far worse things than this.

And she *will* get over it. I'm certain she will.

Takes time, that's all. Just a matter of time.

(Pause.)

The house has been on the market a year.

I've dropped the asking price three times, now.

There's no one coming to look at it at all.

For the moment, she's gone back living with her mum.

Still, the main thing is to stay positive. Right?

There's a buyer for everything, so they say.

And when I *do* sell it, we'll buy something else with an *even better* garden than this.

She'll come back then, won't she?

Of course she will.

(Pause.)

Just a matter of time.

(Fade.)

Norman remembers life in the trenches

Over By Christmas

Over By Christmas was first presented by
East Lane Theatre Company at
East Lane Theatre, Wembley, London

on 23 August 2015
with the following cast:

Norman ... **Chris Wilson**

Norman – *An old man.*

(Norman sits at a small table, sipping beer.
He puts down the glass, stares ahead.)
(Pause.)

NORMAN: My first reaction to the outbreak of war was really a blank.

A total blank. I didn't really see how it could affect me.

(Small chuckle.) Ridiculous, really, looking back now.

I was seventeen years old and working as a clerk in a corn merchant's office. It was no great shakes but my parents were pleased I'd a whitecollar job. That is, as opposed to working down the pit. Well, one day at work, a friend phoned me up.

'What are you doing about the war? I've joined my brother's regiment,' he said. 'If you come along at lunchtime, I'll get you in too.'

Well, up until then, I'd given it no thought. But that's what happened.

I just went along. When I got there, there were hundreds of men.

Perhaps a thousand waiting to enlist. Like a carnival, really.

That's what it was like. 'Be over by Christmas,' some of them said.

(Pause.)

The poster was everywhere. On every building.

There was no escaping the finger and eyes. The pointing finger.

(Points.) Your country needs *you.* Your country needs *you.*

And you. And you. And the women were mostly for it as well.

'Why aren't you in Khaki?' Not all women, though.

No, my girl wasn't for it. Didn't want me to go.

She was dead against it. Right from the start. If I'd listened to her, I would never have gone. If I'd listened to her, I … *(Breaks off.)*

(Pause.)

Hazel eyes and golden hair. I'd been courting her for nearly a year.

She smiled her smile, lit up a room.

(Pause.)

Golden girl.

(Pause.)

It was over quite quick. The recruiting, I mean.

My friend introduced me to the sergeant.

'How old are you?'

'Seventeen and one month,' I said.

He said, 'Don't you mean nineteen? Nineteen, one month?'

The next thing I knew, I was taking the oath.

The next thing I knew, we were all marching off.

What a send off they gave us!

Brass bands playing … the whole town cheering as we marched past.

Sun shining away. Not a cloud in the sky.

Mum and dad in the crowd too, proud as punch.

(Pause.)

Over by Christmas. Christmas. Yes.

They soon changed their minds.

Oh, they changed their minds sharp when we got in the trenches.

Saw what was in store. A different story, then.

(Pause.)

Seems like yesterday sometimes.

The muck and the mud … and the rats.

Yes, everywhere. Everywhere, rats. Not like English rats, no.

As big as cats. Well, they seemed much bigger, anyway. Yes …

We were in this one trench for God knows how long.

The German trench was seventy yards away.

Seventy yards is not much. No distance at all.

But it might as well have been seventy miles.

Our orders were just to *hold position.*

In other words, stay put. That's what we did.

It seemed like we'd be there for the rest of the war.

Bored out of our minds, soaking wet and cold …

And the rain kept coming. Day after day.

You were standing in water up to your waist.

Of course, trench foot was rife. That happened when the mud soaked through your boots and your toes rotted off.

One mate lost two toes. Another lost three.

Trenchfoot Tony, they called him. God! What a life!

But I had her letters. They kept me going.

The one thing that kept me going. Oh yes, her letters kept coming.

Really nice letters about what we'd do when I came home on leave.

When I came home on leave, we went out to the pictures.

We walked in the park if the weather was kind.

Then her parents invited me round there for tea!

A *real* step forward. *The uniform,* you see?

But the leave didn't last long. I was soon back again.

The conditions on the Somme were worse than before.

When the order came to go over the top we were so bloody glad to get out of that trench. So over we went and ... over we went and ...

COMMANDING OFFICER'S VOICE OVER: *(Barks command.)* Walk! That's an Order! Walk! Don't run! Walk towards the enemy in a straight line!

(Briskly reassuring.) The Hun's nearly finished, chaps.

On his last legs. Our preliminary bombardment's

all but polished him off. When he sees you advance
he'll soon beat a retreat.

(Commands.) So *walk!*

NORMAN: So we walked. That's what we did.
Walked.

(Angrily.) Lambs to the bloody slaughter.

(Sudden loud machine gun fire is heard.

*Battle sounds grow louder then gradually fade with
the lights, leaving NORMAN in spotlight.)*

(Silence.)

I was in the ditch three days and three nights.

I thought I would die there. I really did.

I don't really remember how they found me.

They heard *faint groaning.* That's what they said.

They just heard me groaning and pulled me out.

Don't remember much about that.

(Pause.)

I was in the hospital nearly five months.

When I was ready, they sent me back home.

By the time I got home she'd gone and got married.

A shotgun wedding to an older bloke in a reserved
occupation.

He couldn't be called up.

I found out later she thought I was dead.

Well, so many men died. She thought I'd died too.

She convinced herself I wasn't coming back.

(Small chuckle.) A shotgun wedding. You can't argue with that.

(Pause.)

One of those things.

(Pause.)

I never got married. There's been one or two women but no, I've never walked down the aisle.

My girl's still alive. Still lives round here, somewhere.

Sometimes I spot her. Her husband's long dead.

I still hear her voice sometimes. Stroke her hair.

(Pause.)

None of it matters now.

(Fade.)

Sound Effects

1. ***Commanding Officer's Voice Over:***

Brisk, upper class.

2. ***Machine Gun Fire / Battle Sounds:***

Briefly loud, becoming distant, fading with light.

Author's Note

In the event of sound effects not being used:

1. Norman to also read The Commanding Officer's dialogue.

2. The lights fade, as indicated, on to Norman in spotlight.

STANDING ALONE

'Bright blue. Sky blue. It stood out in a crowd. That was half the trouble. It stood out too much.'

The Balaclava

The Balaclava was first presented at The Pump House Theatre, Watford,

on 22 March 2015
with the following cast:

Renton ... **Melville Lovatt**

Renton – *A man in his late forties.*

(Lights up. RENTON sits in a prison cell.
He refers to audience.)

RENTON: Mum spent weeks knitting my balaclava.

A balaclava helmet for my first day at school. Yes a *balaclava.*

A funny sort of word. Bright blue. Sky blue. It stood out in a crowd.

That was half the trouble. It stood out *too* much.

If she'd made it dark blue, it wouldn't have stood out.

Would have just *blended in.* Blended in with the crowd.

Other boys wore them too but theirs were all dark.

Dark blue. Dark grey. Mostly navy blue or black.

I can hear mum's voice, now. 'This'll keep your ears warm through the winter. Your ears will be warm as toast.'

Well, the first school day came. Mum walked me to school.

In those days there were very few cars.

The bus service was hopeless, so everyone walked.

I felt part of an army, marching to school.

And my ears *did* feel warm. No doubt about that.

(Pause)

Our first teacher was Miss Hope. A kindly woman

with a well spoken voice and arthritic hands. We were given colouring books and lots of crayons to colour in all the pictures in the books.

Then she held a competition. A colouring competition.

We did this all morning. I quite enjoyed that.

At the end, she held my colouring book up high and announced me the winner. I was proud as Punch.

(Pause.)

Then the playtime bell rang. Everyone out.

We were out in the playground in no time at all.

I remember the noise. The incredible noise of excited children.

A beautiful noise. Well, to my ears it was at any rate. Yes.

(Small chuckle.) My mum used to say it was a terrible *din.*

I remember I watched older boys play football.

We younger boys weren't allowed to join in.

Fair enough. We were small. Too small to join in.

If I'd gone home, injured, mum would have gone spare.

(Pause.)

As it happened, she wasn't pleased anyway. No.

When she came to collect me, she wasn't pleased at all.

'Where's your balaclava? Where's your balaclava? Where is it?'

'I've lost it. I've lost it,' I said.

'You've lost it? *Lost it?* Well, damned well find it!

I've spent over three and a half weeks knitting that!

Just wait 'til your dad hears. Wait 'til I tell him.

Just wait 'til your dad hears about this, my lad.'

(Pause.)

Sure enough, dad was angry. He'd been betting on the horses.

Turned out, he'd lost most of his wages that day.

He'd been drinking as well. Been drowning his sorrows.

He'd had a bad day. Now, to cap it all off ...

(Chuckles.) To cap it all off!

(Straight faced again.) No, it wasn't funny.

The beating with his belt wasn't funny at all.

My arse was so sore, couldn't sit down for a week.

No, what am I saying? It was more like a month.

(Pause.)

Miss Hope saw me standing. 'Why don't you sit down?'

She kept on asking, 'Why don't you sit down?'

In the end, I just told her. I wish that I hadn't.

Looking back, I wish I'd just made something up.

Got my dad into trouble. A whole lot of trouble.

The NSPCC got involved with it all. Everyone knew about it.

Everyone in our street. My parents were shamed.

Well and truly.

(Pause.)

Dad said he was sorry. I know he was.

I know they both loved me. Deep down, they did.

Mum cried and swore it would never happen again.

(Pause.)

It never did.

(Pause.)

What I didn't tell them, though, was *how* I'd lost it.

I just found I couldn't ... couldn't tell my mum that.

What had happened was this boy, Graham Hall, without any warning, snatched it out of my hand.

Started shouting, 'Soppy colour for a very soppy boy!'

The next thing was, he'd flushed it down the loo.

Well, I couldn't tell mum *that.* I mean, all her hard work ...

Besides, Graham Hall belonged to a gang and they said if I told anyone what had happened, they'd flush my head down the loo as well.

(Pause.)

I often wonder, looking back, how things would have gone if I'd just told the truth.

I mean, would it have made any difference at all?

It's pointless, anyway, looking back.

My guess is my parents would have gone to the school and demanded Graham's parents pay for it. Yes.

But I think dad would still have given me a beating

and told me, 'Next time, just stand up for yourself.'

(Pause.)

Just before mum died, quite a few years later, her mind was wandering all over the place.

'We'd never have split up if that hadn't happened.

That balaclava was the final straw.'

Well, it's true they split up soon after that.

I grew up seeing very little of my dad.

They'd have split up *anyway*. Sooner or later.

(Emphatic.) The point is she was deluding herself.

(Pause.)

Once, for quite a few weeks, mum wore dark glasses.

She never took these dark glasses off.

Sunglasses in winter. Other boys asked me why.

'I've a bad eye infection.

Just tell them that.'

(Pause.)

In spite of everything, when my dad left, I found I missed him. Missed him a lot.

He *could* be gentle. Sometimes *very* gentle.

Used to buy me toy soldiers. Sit me on his knee ...

(Pause.)

Mum never *said* so in so many words, but I know she blamed me for them both splitting up.

There was no ... no way they'd have stayed together.

(Angrily, between small sobs.) No ... *no way.*

Just no way at all!

(He sobs quietly, briefly.

He quickly wipes his eyes.

He looks up, stares ahead.)

(Pause.)

(Evenly.) I'm a pharmacist, now, with a struggling small business.

I set out to deliver some medication to an old man unable to collect it from the shop.

The day had been tiring. The shop, very hot.

I decided, on the way, to stop off for a pint.

Just one pint of lager. I'm not really a drinker.

And it's rare, very rare I go into a pub.

(Pause.)

The pub was nearly empty. Very few people.

I think I recognised him straightaway.

The thing was, he'd become a local hero of sorts. He'd played football and cricket for both local teams. Successful in business.

A chain of sports shops. His face never seemed to be out of the news.

(Pause.)

He was sitting at the bar when I went up to order.

I could sense he was trying to remember who I was.

I said nothing to him. Said nothing at all.

'Don't I know you?' he asked.

'Did you ever find your helmet?'

'Did you ever find your balaclava cap?'

Then he just started laughing. Just couldn't stop laughing.

He'd had a few drinks. I realised that.

'And your mother,' he said, 'with those dark glasses. I remember her wearing those to the school and we all thought she was a secret agent!

A secret agent! A bloody spy!'

He laughed. Laughed again. He couldn't stop laughing.

Then, all of a sudden, he went off to the loo.

'When I come back,' he said, 'I'll buy you a drink.'

Well, I didn't wait around until he came back.

I just left. I just drank up and left.

(Pause.)

The reason I'm sitting in this cell, now, is they think I put something in Graham Hall's drink.

If they really believe that, why haven't they charged me?

They haven't a scrap of evidence, that's why.

The closed circuit footage is as clear as mud.

There's no way they can charge me on that.

The barman *thinks* ... only *thinks* he saw me spike Graham's drink when he went to the loo.

His story is Graham came back, took a sip, and just keeled over. Fell off his stool.

(Pause.)

The thing to remember is Graham was pissed.

It's hardly surprising he fell off his stool.

The police, themselves, agree he was wasted, but they're saying he was poisoned as well.

(Pause.)

This barman's dodgy. Take it from me.

They're holding *him* for further questioning too.

It seems Graham actually *owned* this pub.

They'd both had a huge row the previous day.

(Pause.)

Graham's still in a coma. A kind of coma.

The chances are fifty-fifty, they say.

But the idea I would do anything like that with his drink is too ridiculous for words!

It's true I didn't like him. I never liked him.

But I bore him no malice or any kind of grudge.

We were kids, for God's sake. We were just ... just kids.

Revenge? Too ridiculous for words.

(Fade.)

STANDING ALONE

'Like most men, I suppose I have to confess it's a mystery to me how a woman's mind works.'

The Fishing Trip

The Fishing Trip was first presented at
The Pump House Theatre, Watford,

on 22 March 2015
with the following cast:

Steve ... **Melville Lovatt**

Steve – *A man in his late thirties.*

(Lights up. STEVE is sitting at a small table. He sips coffee, looks straight ahead.)

STEVE: Like most men, I suppose I have to confess it's a mystery to me how a woman's mind works. Perhaps it's just *me* but I don't think it is.

There's millions of men all in the same boat.

Then I read there are some men who don't have a problem because they have extra ... *empathy.* Right? A nice sounding word. I wasn't sure what it meant. So I looked it up. And there it was.

The power to imaginatively enter into another person's feelings.

Well, this cheered me up. I always believed I could do that, you see.

With Donna. Well ... I was wrong.

(Pause.)

(The stage darkens. The lighting is now more subdued.)

All three of us, Ron and Jack Reynolds and me, had been looking forward to the fishing trip for months. It was something we did just once a year. An annual event. Our dream come true!

Yes, four days fishing. Our idea of heaven.

No work. No wives. No children. No mess.

Just us and the river. The fish in the river.

(Pause.)

Four days bliss.

(Pause.)

The weather was good too, when we set out. Sun shining.

Quite warm for the time of the year. We set out with our tents and enough food and drink to sink a battleship. Whisky and beer ... Jack loved his whisky.

Just couldn't get enough. Still, it has to be said, he caught the most fish.

The more pissed he became, the more fish he caught.

(Reflects.) Always *was* a lucky old sod ...

(Pause.)

It was Ron who spotted her.

There we were. We'd just set up our rods and pitched up our tents.

Everything was set up for the next four days.

'What's that?' he said. 'There? Over there?'

(Pause.)

From that distance ... I would say about twenty yards away ... it wasn't clear what we were looking at. No. She was partly hidden by the curve of the bank and the trees. The bushes and trees.

(Pause.)

My immediate thoughts were *we've got to go back.*

Go back and report it to the police straightaway.

(Emphatic.) I *told* them. I said, 'We've *got* to go back.'

(Pause.)

They didn't see it like that.

(Pause.)

We were tired from walking the two miles from the van.

'This is our treat,' Ron said. 'Our treat, once a year. The girl's dead.

She's not going anywhere,' he said.

(Pause.)

Well, this was true.

(Pause.)

'Besides,' Jack said. 'What difference will it make if we report it now or in four days' time?' We drank whisky. Talked about it. From every angle.

The key question was *what difference would it make?*

'She's dead,' Ron kept saying. 'There's nothing we can do,' Jack's saying.

Over and over again. The next thing we knew ... the light was going.

Only quarter past four and already going dark.

Too dark to start walking back to the van. Well, no, not *really,* but ... anyway, well, we decided to leave it until the next day.

Like I said, it was their two votes to my one.

I was far from happy but what could I do?

(Pause.)

What could I do?

(Pause.)

In the morning we covered the same ground again.

Ron and Jack were the same. They wanted to stay and finish the fishing.

I wanted to go. But I couldn't see how I could go without them.

So we talked and we drank more whisky and beer.

Ron suggested we cut the trip short by a day.

Instead of four days, we settle for three?

We settle for three days instead of four?

(Pause.)

So that's what we did.

(Pause.)

We secured the body so it wouldn't float away.

We tied the wrists of the body to a bush.

When we told the police this, they took a dim view.

Said we should have left the body alone.

They were right, of course, but we'd acted for the best.

In the end they could see we'd acted for the best.

When all's said and done, we had nothing to hide.

(Emphatic.) The point is, we'd done nothing wrong.

(Pause.)

When I finally came home, it was quarter past three.

I knew Donna wouldn't thank me for waking her up.

I was drained … exhausted from talking to the police.

(Pause.)

So I just let her sleep.

(Pause.)

I just slid into bed. Slipped under the bedclothes, next to her.

Quiet. As quiet as a mouse. I could just hear her breathing, shallow and soft.

(Pause.)

She slept like a log.

(Pause.)

I lay on my back. No way could *I* sleep.

I kept seeing the girl. Kept seeing her hair.

Her hair on the water. Floating on top.

Her beautiful long blonde hair.

(Pause.)

Then out of the blue, Donna turned in her sleep.

She just turned. Turned towards me ... only semi-awake.

And she kissed me and started saying she'd missed me.

Okay, I *had* been away three days, but the thing was, it wasn't ... it wasn't as if ... well, we'd reached a point where we hardly made love, and never, no *never* in the middle of the night.

(Pause.)

It made a nice change.

(Pause.)

Afterwards, I remember thinking things *will* be

better from this point on. She still ... still loves me. I still love her.

There's nothing between us which can't ... be fixed.

There's nothing between us which can't be resolved.

I remember ... thinking that.

(Pause.)

I must have slept for seven hours. When I woke, I could hear her downstairs on the phone. I couldn't make out the words.

I got up, went downstairs. She handed me the phone.

'It's for you. It's The Brinkley Gazette.'

(Pause.)

And the next thing was, we were *in* The Gazette.

Three local fishermen find murdered girl.

A few days' later, they made an arrest.

They charged this guy with murder and rape.

Ex boyfriend. She'd left him for somebody else.

(Pause.)

He went down for life.

(Pause.)

I still can't see how I did anything wrong.

That's not how she saw it. Donna, that is.

'Why didn't you tell the police straightaway?

And you never told *me*, and then we made love.'

She just couldn't ... *wouldn't* leave it ... leave it alone.

(Pause.)

She wouldn't leave it alone.

(Pause.)

Then she went to the funeral. The girl's funeral.

She said she *had to. Had to go.*

She didn't *know* the girl. The girl was a stranger.

Donna never knew her. Strange but true, she insisted she *had* to go to the funeral.

(Pause.)

What can you say?

(Pause.)

I've never known what to make of it, really.

From the funeral onwards, everything changed.

She came back, a changed woman. A different woman.

I couldn't get through to her. Ever again.

It became an obsession. 'How could you leave her? How could you carry on fishing, like that'?

'Look, the girl was dead,' I kept telling her. *'Dead.'*

(Pause.)

Things were never the same.

(Pause.)

I still ... still love her. I still think we can ... if she'll only come back, we can still make it work. The point ... the point is, we were married twelve years. Twelve years together. Through thick and through thin. Okay, in twelve years, people have ups and downs.

But we stayed ... together. That's got to mean ...

well ... well, that's got to mean *something.* Well *I* think it does.

(Pause.)

Don't you think it does?

(Pause.)

Since Donna left, I've had more time for fishing.

But I've gone right off it, to tell you the truth.

It's the same with Ron and the same with Jack.

(Pause.)

Now we play golf instead.

(Fade.)

STANDING ALONE

'The thing is, I still love her. She knows I still love her. I've never not loved her. She knows ... knows that. It was just ... for a year ... I thought I ... well ... I thought I loved Inga too.'

Access

Access was first presented as part of
The Jubilee Arts Culture
Harrow May Day Celebrations by
Belmont Theatre Company
at The Harrow Heritage Centre

on 6 May 2002
with the following cast:

Marshall ... **Graham Broderick**

Marshall – *A man in his forties.*

(Lights up. MARSHALL sits by a small round table.
He is drinking wine, stares ahead.
Pause.
He slowly refills his glass.)

MARSHALL: *(Refers to audience, offers bottle.)* Are you sure you won't have a drink? Just one?
(Puts down bottle.) Alright then, right you are.
(Pause.)
Today I took the girls to the pictures. Harry Potter. They loved it, they did. They loved it. Both of them. That made a change. The first time we've been to a film they've *both* liked.
(Pause. Marshall takes a cigarette from packet, decides against lighting it, puts it back.)
Next Sunday we'll have to do something different.
There's nothing else on that's suitable, then. Besides, I've flogged the cinema to death the last three Sundays. Three?
No, four. The thing is, when it's raining, it takes some beating.
And Christine *never* takes them to films so when I suggest it, they're always thrilled. Still, variety's the name of the game.
I think, next week, I'll take them to Madame Tussaud's and The Planetarium. That's the best bet. They'll both like it there.

I'm sure they will. I'll steer clear of The Chamber Of Horrors, though. Yes.

No, I won't take them there. I'll give that a wide berth. I don't want them having nightmares, poor dears. And Christine wouldn't thank me.

Wouldn't thank me for that.

(Pause.)

That's *all* we need.

(Pause.)

One Sunday, I ... about two months ago ... I took them on a boat in Hyde Park. Lovely day, it was. Gorgeous. Sun shining away on the Serpentine. Just the day for a sail. The thing was, though, I found it hard going at first. Just rowing the boat. Sounds pathetic, I know. But I'm out of condition. I haven't rowed for years. The girls were both laughing.

Highly amused. Still, I know they enjoyed it. They both said they did.

(Pause.)

That's the main thing.

(Pause.)

After the boat ride, I sat them both down on a bench and went off to buy them ice creams. I was gone ... *(Shrugs.)* three minutes?

Well, no more than that. Then when I came back, I'd a bit of a shock.

There's this old woman there. An *oldish* woman. With a policeman.

Well, she starts pointing at *me*. 'That's him,' she

kept saying.

'That's him. That's the man.' The policeman just stared at me.

'That's him,' she said. It turned out she thought I'd just picked up the girls to buy them ice creams and do horrible things. A real nutcase, she was.

'I'm their father,' I said. The policeman just stared.

I said, 'Look, I'm their dad.' In the end, the policeman just said he was sorry.

The woman made no apology at all. Stupid bat. I mean, okay, I needed a shave.

I'd overslept and had no time to shave. So, okay, I looked rough, but not *that* rough.

(Incredulous, small chuckle.) No need to call the police.

(Pause.)

When I took the girls back, they told Christine about it. They told her.

'The woman was nutty,' they said. Well, Christine just stared at me.

Just for a second, I thought she just might … invite me in. But, no. No such luck.

Just the usual words. *(Mimics Christine's voice.)* 'Say goodbye to dad.'

(Pause.)

(He gulps down wine, quickly refills glass, leans forward, stares ahead.)

One of these Sundays she *will* let me in. She's still … still bitter.

That's all ... it is. She's a right to be bitter, I know.
Know that.

(Pause.)

She's a right to be mad.

(Pause.)

What is it they say? Time heals all wounds? *(Nods.)*
I'm sure that's true.

I'm sure she'll come round. The point is this sort of
thing happens all the time.

Couples split up for six months or a year, then get
back together. Start over again.

(Pause.)

Happens all the time.

(Pause.)

She's been badly hurt. I realise that. I still don't
know why I did what I did.

Looking back, I must have been off my trolley. I
suppose I just didn't ... just didn't stop to think.
Well, I've learned my lesson now. Well and truly.

She *knows* I still love her. That's the main thing.
When all's said and done we were married ten
years.

(Pause.)

Ten very good years.

(Pause.)

Oh sure, those ten years, there were good times
and bad.

Like any marriage ... there's ups and downs. But all
told, we were happy.

The girls were happy. When they were born our lives were complete.

Nice house. Good jobs. Lots of holidays abroad. Those holidays ... yes ... terrific, they were. Majorca. Minorca. South of France. Crete.

I think Crete was my favourite. Christine preferred France.

Camping out in France. The girls loved all that too.

Helping me fix up the tent ...

(Pause.)

(He quickly wipes a tear, refills his glass.)

The thing is, I still love her. She *knows* I still love her. I've never *not* loved her.

She knows ... knows that. It was just ... for a year ... I thought I ... well,

(Shrugs.) I thought I loved Inga too.

(Pause.)

This sort of thing happens. Goes on all the time.

(Shrugs.) Christine asked me to choose.

Choose Inga or her. But I couldn't. Couldn't choose. I loved ... them both.

(Pause.)

I found I couldn't choose.

(Pause.)

So one day Christine said, 'You'd better move out. You'd better move out and go live with her.' She just wouldn't ... wouldn't have it any other way.

(Pause.)

So that's what I did.

(Pause.)

At first it was fine. A brand new life. I can't say I missed my old life at all.

I didn't really miss the kids for the first nine months. Seems incredible now, but that's how it was. And the sex was fantastic with Inga.

Oh yes, she couldn't get enough. *(Small chuckle.)* Real nympho she was.

First thing in the morning and last thing at night. And not just in the bedroom.

Everywhere else. On the kitchen table. In front of the fire. In the garden.

The garage. The staircase. The loo. *(Reflects.)* The only place we *didn't* do it was up on the roof … I just wanted it all to go on and on.

And it seemed like it would. I was sure that it would.

I had no reason to think that it wouldn't.

We were happy together. Inga seemed very happy. Okay, we had some separate interests, it's true … she had some separate interests. I had some too.

(Offers bottle.) Are you *sure* you won't have a drink?

(Pause.)

(He puts bottle down.)

Well, one weekend Inga had to fly out to Antwerp. 'An important business conference,' she said. She was gone a week. *(Small chuckle.)* I was glad of the break. But when she came back, I knew. Just *knew*.

Three weeks later ... just before my divorce ... how's that for timing?

She said, 'That was it.' Said, 'We haven't much in common. Things haven't worked out.' She was going to live with some guy she'd met ...

Unbelievable, really. I couldn't ... believe it. Soon after that, she was gone.

(Pause.)

The next thing was, I was making mistakes. At work. My concentration was zilch. At first they were good. Said, 'You just need a rest. Why not take some time off to sort yourself out?' So that's what I did. I took some time off.

(Pause.)

I'm still taking time off.

(Pause.)

But this *can't* go on, can it? Every Sunday like this? It's ridiculous.

Too ridiculous for words. Christine knows I still love her.

She *knows ... knows that.* This guy she's just met ... it won't ... won't *last.*

(Scoffs.) She tells me she loves him. Do me a favour. What is he? A toy boy!

A toy boy, that's all! Let her have her affair. I'll be here when he's gone.

She'll have had her affair, like I've had mine. Then we'll get back together.

Be a family again.

(Pause.)

A family again.
(Fade.)

STANDING ALONE

*'He's coming. You'll be pleased to know
I've invited him to your funeral.'*

Monologue

Monologue was first presented as part of the
Jubilee Arts Culture
Harrow May Day Celebrations by
Belmont Theatre Company at
The Harrow Heritage Centre

On 6 May 2002
with the following cast:

Man ... **Bill Baynes**

Man – *In his mid-fifties.*

(In a pool of light, stage centre, closed coffin on top of a table.

By coffin, a chair. MAN sitting in chair. He is in his mid-fifties.

He stares ahead.)

(Silence.)

MAN: *(Refers to coffin.)* He's coming. You'll be pleased to know I've invited him to your funeral. I thought ... you'd approve.

You'd want him there. Anyway, it's arranged. Yes. Phoned him up yesterday. Got his number out of your little black book.

Flabbergasted, he was. Seemed a nice enough bloke.

A Yorkshire man, eh?

(Pause.)

Had quite a chat.

(Silence.)

Just been out with the dog. I felt like a stroll. Quite nice out now.

Nice and fresh. Just set off walking. Nearly got lost.

Ended up in the woods by the stream. *(Small chuckle.)* Uh. Seemed like yesterday. Still the same old place. Strange we never went back.

I mean, all this time ... twenty years. Twenty-five years.

You'd have thought …

(Pause.)

Green. Those days you always wore green. Green shoes, green dress, green … everything green. My favourite colour. You wore it for me.

You used to say …

(Pause.)

Took it off for me too. There. Then. On the grass. By the stream.

The sun through the trees. 'Hold the moment,' you said.

'Forever,' you said.

(Pause.)

As if we could.

(Pause.)

As if we could ever. Stupid bitch. Fleeting. Fleeting.

The whole bloody thing. The whole stinking pantomime.

Day? Night? Hold on to the moment? Balls.

(Pause.)

There were fish in the stream. We lay on the bank.

We didn't smoke in those days, did we? No.

Incidentally, I've stopped. Since you died I've managed to kick it completely. No sweat at all. Well, I missed them at first, but now … that's it. No cough. No wheezing. Gone.

(Pause.)

The grass was parched. Hadn't rained for weeks.

Must have been in the eighties. You wanted to swim.

Wished the stream was the sea. You closed your eyes and wished for the sea. May. Yes, it was May. Late May.

The first really good weather we'd had that year. Everything was still.

The leaves. The grass. The sky. All still. Only the stream ... moved.

(Pause.)

And the fish in the stream. I picked up a pebble to throw at the fish.

I wanted them gone. Wanted *everything* still. You took my hand.

Took the pebble from my hand.

(Pause.)

What does he do? For a living, I mean? An actor? Something to do with the arts? Came across quite arty. On the phone.

Had a drama school type of voice.

(Pause.)

By the way, don't worry yourself about *me.*

I've a bit on the side as well, pet. *(Nods.)* Yes. My own little fling.

I'm screwing her Mondays, Tuesdays, Fridays ... *Fridays* are best.

That's variety night. You name it. The floor. Outside on the lawn.

On top of the fridge. It's been going on ages. You

never knew?

Don't worry yourself over me.

(Pause.)

Sometimes it's the car. We go for a drive. Drive out to The George.

Your favourite pub. Yes, the good old George. They've tarted it up a bit but it's basically still the same. Same bar. Same beams.

Same beer. Same clock. We sit by the fire. Watch the flames.

I sip my beer. She sips your drink.

(Pause.)

She sits in your chair.

(Pause.)

Once we went to The Swan. That's changed completely.

Plastic. All plastic. Not the same place. Flashing lights. Jukebox.

God. What a din. No thanks. Give me The George.

(Pause.)

She always wears green. She sits in your chair. Her eyes are open.

They never close. They never close except when she sleeps.

Her eyes are open for *me.*

(Pause.)

We rarely talk. No need for words. We lie by the stream.

The sun through the trees. Everything silent except for the stream.

(Pause.)

The fish in the stream.

(Pause.)

The sun on her hair. She smiles her smile. Everything silent.

No words at all. Her smile, for me. I watch her hair.

(Pause.)

Everything still.

(Pause.)

Sometimes we walk. Just walk for miles across the fields or down the lanes. Our footsteps ... breathing together ... one. No destination ... walking on ... she smiling her smile, her smile for *me*.

(Pause.)

I love you I said.

(Pause.)

Sheffield, his town. Passed through there once. Took the wrong turning off the M1. Peak District first. No time to stop.

Ended up in the town. A nightmare it was. Drove around in a circle.

Couldn't get out. No signs. Nothing. Couldn't find my way out.

Picked up a hitch hiker. Showed me the way. Long time ago now.

Rough. Yes. She likes it rough. I ride her hard. I give it her rough.

I make her squeal. Most times it's rough. Sometimes it's slow.

(Shouts.) Don't worry yourself over me!

(Pause.)

(Softer.) Threw it away. Threw the pebble away.

Lay back in the grass and closed your eyes. Wished again for the sea.

Your eyes like ... no ... keeping me ... no ... shutting me ... no ...

Even then? *No.* You loved me then. Much later ... in Spain ... Madrid ... that ... yes ... much later ... Madrid ... your eyes ... closed.

(Pause.)

(Closes eyes, soft.) Shutting me out.

(Pause.)

(Evenly.) Incidentally, how old is he? Thirty-five?

I'd have said mid-thirties. Could be wrong.

Sounded young on the phone, he ... *very young.*

I'd have put him mid-twenties. *Knowing you.*

I mean, you liked them young, didn't you?

Half your age? The younger the better.

(Sobs, thrashes coffin with fists.) You filthy slag you lousy rotten cow I'll dance on your grave I'll dance I'll dance I'll ...

(Sobbing, he slumps across coffin. Sobbing stops. Silence.

He slumps back in chair.)

The forecast is good for tomorrow. Good. Scattered

showers at first, then sunny all day. *(Looks out ahead.)* There's a red sky now for you.

Over there. All day through 'til evening ... sun.

(Fade.)

www.ingramcontent.com/pod-product-compliance
Lightning Source LLC
Chambersburg PA
CBHW060352090426
42734CB00011B/2120